TEN GREAT EVENTS IN HISTORY

TEN GREAT EVENTS IN HISTORY

COMPILED AND ARRANGED

By **JAMES JOHONNOT**

GYAN

Published by

Gyan Publishing House
5, Ansari Road
Daryaganj, New Delhi-110002
Phone: 011-47034999, 9811692060
E-mail: books@gyanbooks.com

Distribution Network
gyanbooks.com
India, USA, Canada, UK, Australia, France

ISBN : 978-81-212-6424-2 (PB)
First Published, 1887

2nd Impression 2022

Printed at: Gyan Press, Delhi.

TEN GREAT EVENTS IN HISTORY
Author: JAMES JOHONNOT

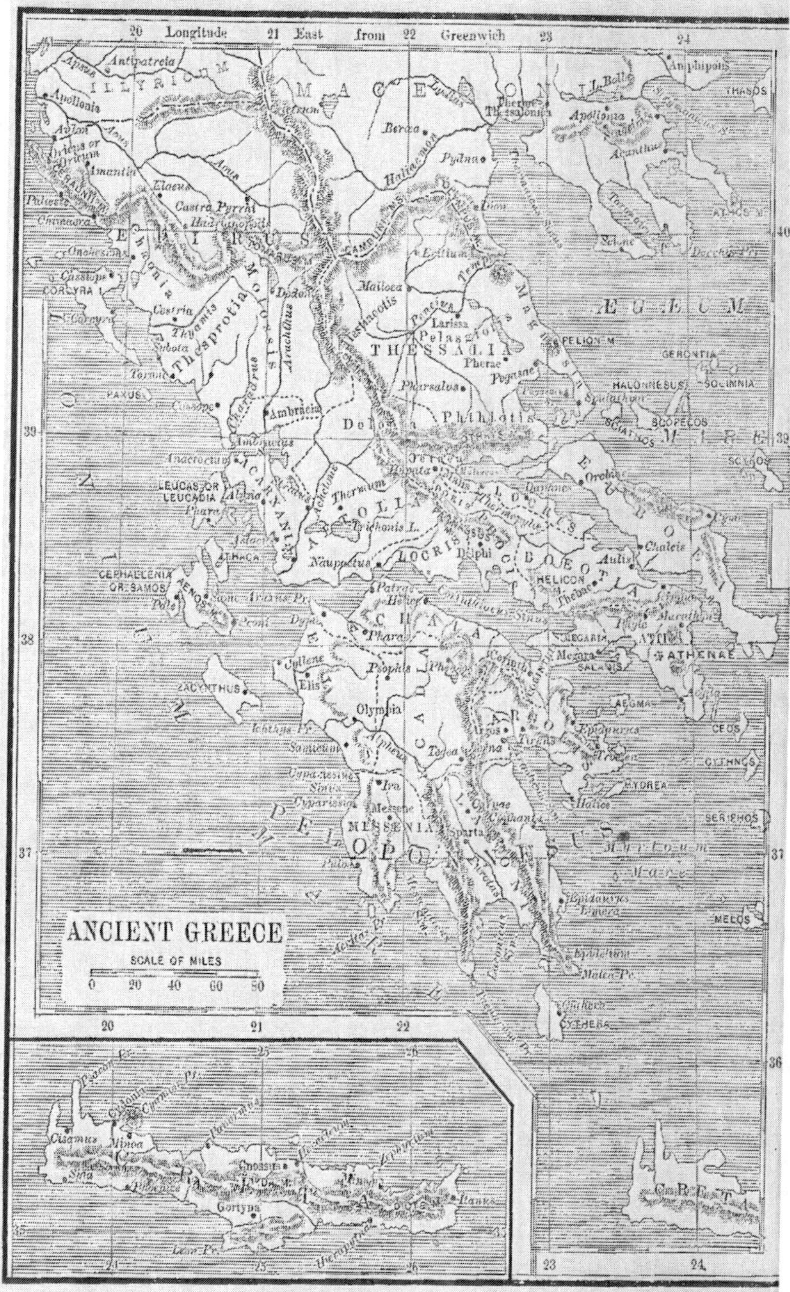
20 Longitude 21 East from 22 Greenwich 23 24
ILLYRICUM
MACEDONIA
Apollonia
Antipatreia
Amphipolis
THASOS
Thessalonica
Beraea
Pydna
Haliacmon
EPIRUS
CORCYRA I.
Chaonia
Thesprotia
Molossis
Dodona
Ambracia
THESSALIA
Larissa
Pelasgiotis
Pherae
Pagasae
Pharsalus
PELION M.
Phthiotis
Dolopia
HALONNESUS
SCOPELOS
PAXUS
LEUCAS OR LEUCADIA
ACARNANIA
AETOLIA
Thermum
Trichonis L.
ITHACA
CEPHALLENIA OR SAMOS
Naupactus
LOCRIS
Delphi
BOEOTIA
HELICON
Thebae
Aulis
Chalcis
MEGARIS
Megara
SALAMIS
ATTICA
ATHENAE
ACHAIA
Patrae
Corinth
ZACYNTHUS
Cyllene
Elis
Olympia
Psophis
ARCADIA
ARGOLIS
Argos
Tiryns
Tegea
Epidaurus
AEGINA
CEOS
CYTHNOS
HYDREA
SERIPHOS
Ira
Messene
MESSENIA
Sparta
PELOPONNESUS
MELOS
CYTHERA
ANCIENT GREECE
SCALE OF MILES
0 20 40 60 80
Cisamus
Minoa
Cnossus
Gortyna
CRETA
38
37
36

TEN GREAT EVENTS IN HISTORY

COMPILED AND ARRANGED

By JAMES JOHONNOT

1887

PREFACE.

Patriotism, or love of country, is one of the tests of nobility of character. No great man ever lived that was not a patriot in the highest and truest sense. From the earliest times, the sentiment of patriotism has been aroused in the hearts of men by the narrative of heroic deeds inspired by love of country and love of liberty. This truth furnishes the key to the arrangement and method of the present work. The ten epochs treated are those that have been potential in shaping subsequent events, and when men have struck blows for human liberty against odds and regardless of personal consequences. The simple narrative carries its own morals, and the most profitable work for the teacher will be to merely supplement the narrative so that the picture presented shall be all the more vivid. Moral reflections are wearisome and superfluous.

CONTENTS.

CHAPTER PAGE

I.—Defense of Freedom by Greek Valor . . 7

II.—Crusades and the Crusaders . . . 24

III.—Defense of Freedom in Alpine Passes . . 59

IV.—Bruce and Bannockburn 83

V.—Columbus and the New World . . . 117

VI.—Defense of Freedom on Dutch Dikes . . 145

VII.—The Invincible Armada 166

VIII.—Freedom's Voyage to America . . . 196

IX.—Plassey; And how an Empire was Won . . 220

X.—Lexington and Bunker Hill . . . 244

TEN GREAT EVENTS IN HISTORY.

CHAPTER I.

DEFENSE OF FREEDOM BY GREEK VALOR.

1. The great events in history are those where, upon special occasions, a man or a people have made a stand against tyranny, and have preserved or advanced freedom for the people. Sometimes tyranny has taken the form of the oppression of the many by the few in the same nation, and sometimes it has been the oppression of a weak nation by a stronger one. The successful revolt against tyranny, the terrible conflict resulting in the emancipation of a people, has always been the favorite theme of the historian, marking as it does a step in the progress of mankind from a savage to a civilized state.

2. One of the earliest as well as most notable of these conflicts of which we have an authentic account took place in Greece twenty-four hundred years ago, or five hundred years before the Christian era. At that time nearly all of Europe was inhabited by rude barbarous tribes. In all that broad land the arts and sciences which denote civilization had made their appearance only in the small and apparently insignificant peninsula of Greece, lying on the extreme southeast border adjoining Asia.

3. At a period before authentic history begins, it is probable that roving tribes of shepherds from the north

took possession of the hills and valleys of Greece. Shut off on the north by mountain ranges, and on all other sides surrounded by the sea, these tribes were able to maintain a sturdy independence for many hundred years. The numerous harbors and bays which subdivide Greece invited to a maritime life, and at a very early time, the descendants of the original shepherds became skillful navigators and courageous adventurers.

4. The voyages of Æneas and Ulysses in the siege of Troy, and those of Jason in search of the golden fleece, and of Perseus to the court of King Minos, are the mythological accounts, embellished by imagination and distorted by time, of what were real voyages. Crossing the Mediterranean, Grecian adventurers became acquainted with the Egyptians, then the most civilized people of the world; and from Egypt they took back to their native country the germs of the arts and sciences which afterward made Greece so famous.

5. Thence improvements went forward with rapid strides. Hints received from Egypt were reproduced in higher forms. Massive temples became light and airy, rude sculpture became beautiful by conforming to natural forms, and hieroglyphics developed into the letters which Cadmus invented or improved. Schools were established, athletic sports were encouraged, æsthetic taste was developed, until in the arts, in philosophy, in science, and in literature the Greeks took the lead of all peoples.

6. As population increased, colonies went out, settling upon the adjacent coasts of Asia and upon the islands farther west. In Asia the Greek colonists were subject to the Persian Empire, which then extended its rule over all Western Asia, and claimed dominion over Africa and Eastern Europe. The Greeks, fresh from the freedom of their native land, could not patiently endure the extor-

tions of the Persian government, to which their own people submitted without question; hence conflicts arose which finally culminated in Persia taking complete possession of the Asiatic Greek cities.

7. But the ties of kinship were strong, and the people of Greece keenly resented the tyranny which had been exercised over their countrymen, and an irrepressible conflict arose between the two nations. The Persian king, Darius, determined to put an end to all annoyance by invading and subjugating Greece. Before the final march of his army, Darius sent heralds throughout Greece demanding soil and water as an acknowledgment of the supremacy of Persia, but Herodotus says that at Sparta, when this impudent demand was made, the heralds were thrown into wells and told to help themselves to all the earth and water they liked.

8. After a long preparation, in 490 B.C., an army of one hundred thousand men or more, under the command of Artaphernes, convoyed by a formidable fleet, invaded Greece. For a long time it met with little opposition, and city after city submitted to the overwhelming hosts of the Persian king. The approach to Athens was regarded as the final turning point of the war.

9. Artaphernes selected the Plains of Marathon, twenty-two miles to the northeast of Athens, as the place of his final landing. His forces, by the lowest estimate, consisted of one hundred and fifty thousand men, of which ten thousand were cavalry. To these were opposed the army of Athens and its allies, consisting in all of ten thousand men. The battle-ground forms an irregular crescent, six miles long and two broad in its widest part. It is bounded on one side by the sea, and on the other by a rampart of mountains. At the time of the battle the extremities of the plain were flanked by

swamps, diminishing the extent of the front, and hampering the operations of the larger army. The command of the Greek army had been intrusted to ten generals, who ruled successively one day each. Themistocles, one of these generals, resigned his day in favor of Miltiades, and all the others followed his example. And so the battle was set, ten thousand Greeks, under Miltiades, against the overwhelming hosts of the enemy.

10. The Persians, confident in their numbers, erected no intrenchments. They did not dream of an attack from the little band of Greeks. There is evidence to believe that they were dissatisfied with the nature of the battle-field they had chosen, and were upon the point of embarking to land at some point nearer the city. If this was the case, they were very rudely awakened from their dream of security by the movement of the Greeks.

11. On the morning of the tenth day after leaving Athens, Miltiades drew up his army in order of battle. He was obliged to perilously weaken his center in order to confront the whole of the Persian army, so as to avoid the danger of being outflanked and surrounded. The Greeks began the battle by a furious attack along the whole line, endeavoring to close in a hand-to-hand conflict as soon as possible, so as to avoid the deadly arrows of the Persians, and to take the advantage of their heavier arms. The Persians were greatly astonished when they saw this little band rushing against them with such a headlong dash, and thought that the Greeks must have been seized with madness. The Persian general had concentrated his forces at the center, and at this part of the battle-field the fiery onset of Greeks was checked by mere weight of numbers. But at length the mighty Persian force moved irresistibly forward, forcing the Greeks slowly backward, fighting, dying, but never yield-

ing. Soon the Greek army were cut in two, and the Persians marched proudly onward to assured victory.

12. But the battle was not yet over. The genius of Miltiades had anticipated this result. The wings of the Greek army, strengthened at the expense of the center, fell upon the weakened wings of the Persians with irresistable onset. The invaders were forced back step by step, the retreat soon changing into a wild and promiscuous rout, and two-thirds of the Persian army ceased to exist as a fighting force. The victorious Greeks now turned their attention to the Persian center, falling upon its flanks with incredible fury. Surrounded on all sides, for a time the Persians maintained their old reputation as valiant soldiers, but nothing could withstand the impetuosity of the Greeks, and soon the whole of the invading hosts were in tumultuous retreat.

13. The victorious Greeks pressed rapidly forward to prevent the foe from embarking, and, if possible, to capture some of the ships. But the Persian archers held the victors in check until the flying soldiery were embarked, and the Greeks obtained possession of only seven vessels. But they were left in undisputed possession of the field of battle, the camp of the enemy, and an immense amount of treasure which had been abandoned in the precipitate flight. Six thousand four hundred Persian dead remained on the plain, while the Greek loss was one hundred and ninety-two.

14. All Athens hastened to welcome the brave soldiery. A Spartan force, on its way to join the Athenians, arrived too late to take part in the battle, and they quietly returned home. As the news spread, loud and frantic rejoicings were heard throughout Greece, and the name of Persia, so long a dread and a menace, lost much of its terrors.

Acropolis at Athens.

15. But the battle of Marathon, and the victory of Miltiades, had a wider significance than could enter into the imaginations of then living man. It was a conflict between the barbarism of Asia and the dawning civilization of Europe, between Oriental despotism and human liberty. The victory rendered normal human growth possible, and, to use the expressive phrase of the modern poet—

> "Henceforth to the sunset, unchecked on its way,
> Shall liberty follow the march of the day."

It was not for the Greeks alone, but for all ages and all peoples; and in this Western World, when we celebrate the birth of our own country, we should ever keep in mind the desperate struggle at Marathon, and the valor of Miltiades and his Greek soldiery.

16. But the war was not yet over. A single defeat did not extinguish the hopes of the Persian monarch, nor exhaust the resources of his empire. Herodotus says: "Now Darius was very bitter against the Athenians, and when he heard the tale of the battle of Marathon he was much more wroth, and desired much more eagerly to march against Hellas. Straightway he sent heralds to all the cities, and bade them make ready an army, and to furnish much more than they had done before, both ships, and horses, and corn; and while the heralds were going round, all Asia was shaken for three years; but in the fourth year the Egyptians, who had been made slaves by Cambyses, rebelled against the Persians, and then the king sought only the more vehemently to go both against the Egyptians and against the Greeks. So he named Xerxes, his son, to be king over the Persians after himself, and made ready to march. But in the year after the revolt of Egypt, Darius himself died; nor was he suffered

to punish the Athenians or the Egyptians who had rebelled against him."

17. The death of Darius gave Greece a respite, but the final conflict was only postponed. Xerxes was weak, obstinate, and vain-glorious, but he inherited all his father's hatred of the Greeks, and he resolved upon one supreme effort to reduce them to subjection. For seven years more the whole vast Persian empire resounded with the notes of preparation. In 480 B. C., ten years after the battle of Marathon, everything was in readiness. A formidable fleet had been built and equipped, corn and military stores had been collected to a vast amount, and an army had gathered which, including camp followers, was variously estimated at from three to five millions. A bridge of boats was built across the Hellespont, and the Oriental horde was prepared to ravage the Grecian valleys like a swarm of devouring locusts. A great storm arose and destroyed the bridge, and the Persian despot ordered the Hellespont scourged with whips in token of his displeasure. When the bridge was rebuilt, Xerxes, from a throne erected upon the shore, for seven days and nights, watched his mighty host pass over from Asia into Europe.

18. In the mean time the Greeks were preparing for the onset. Sparta, true to her military organization, did little but to bring her army to the perfection of discipline, and many of the weaker cities resolved to quietly submit to the invaders. The Athenians alone seemed to have fully understood the gravity of the situation. To them the rage of the Persian king was particularly directed, for the crushing defeat at Marathon, and Athens was more exposed than any other of the Greek cities. During the ten years Athens raised and equipped as large an army as her population would warrant. Every able-

bodied man was enrolled in the ranks. Food and military stores were collected, but the chief means of defense was a novel one, and showed the desperate nature of the conflict in which they were about to engage. Under the wise direction of Themistocles they built a formidable fleet, so large that in case of emergency the whole population of the city could embark, and either remain afloat or take refuge on the neighboring islands.

19. A congress of the cities had determined to oppose the approach of Xerxes at some favorable place by a combined army. At the head of the Maliac gulf there was a narrow pass, through which the Persians had to go, the road running between a mountain and a swamp which stretched to the sea; and at one place the swamp came so near the mountain that there was hardly room for the road to run between. This is the famous pass of Thermopylæ; and here it was that a small army might block the way against any number of the enemy. Across this pass a wall was built, and behind it was posted the Greek army under the command of Leonidas, the Spartan king. His forces consisted of three hundred Spartans, seven hundred Thespians, and about four thousand more from the various Grecian cities. The Persians approached, and for four days waited, expecting to see the Greek army disperse at the very sight of their formidable numbers. But as they were apparently not frightened, on the fifth day the Persians made an attack. For two days the battle continued, inflicting great losses upon the Persians, while the little army of Leonidas, behind their fortifications, was scarcely injured.

20. On the third morning a renegade Greek showed Xerxes a path across the mountains where he could completely turn the Greek position. The Persians were not slow to avail themselves of this intelligence, and toward

the close of the third day Leonidas saw the enemy descending the mountain, ready to surround him and cut

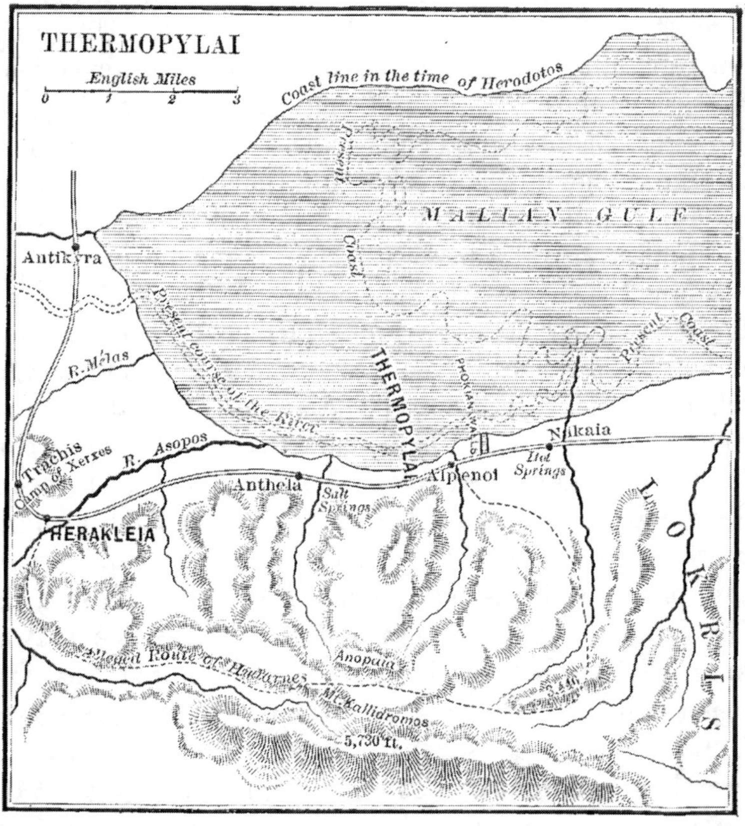

off his retreat. Acting promptly, he ordered his allies to leave the field before it was too late, but he, with his devoted band of three hundred, were to remain, in accordance of a Spartan law which forbade a Spartan soldier ever to retreat from the presence of an enemy. The seven hundred Thespians remained with him, and the whole band was cut down, but not without inflicting fearful loss upon the enemy.

21. While the passage of Thermopylæ was disputed, the Greek fleet advanced and took position in the strait of Artemisium, to prevent the Persian fleet from advancing farther into Greek waters. During the battle the fleets were also engaged in an indecisive conflict. A storm, however, arose and destroyed two hundred of the Persian ships. When Thermopylæ fell there was no longer reason for defending Artemisium, and the Greek fleet returned to defend the approach to Athens at the strait of Salamis.

22. Athens was now at the mercy of the conqueror. The Spartan army moved off to defend their own city. It was now that the wisdom of Themistocles showed itself. "The Athenians had no hope of being able to defend Athens, and resolved to abandon the town, and to remove their wives and children out of Attica to a place of safety. The whole population, men, women, and children, sorrowfully left their homes, and streamed down to the sea-shore, carrying what they could with them." The fleet took them over to Salamis and adjacent islands; and when Xerxes reached Athens he found it silent and deserted. A few poor or desperate men alone refused to depart, and had posted themselves behind a wooden fortification on the top of the Acropolis, the fortress and sanctuary of Athens. The Persians fired the fortifications, stormed the Acropolis, slaughtered its defenders, and burned every holy place to the ground. Athens and its citadel were in the hands of the barbarians; its inhabitants were scattered, its holy places destroyed. One hope alone remained to the Athenians—the ships which Themistocles had persuaded them to build.

23. The fleet was anchored in the strait of Salamis, and beside the two hundred ships of Athens, it consisted of a large number from other ports of Greece. Among

the Greeks there were divided counsels; some were for giving immediate battle, and some were for flying from the thousand Persian ships now advancing upon them. Themistocles saw that to retreat would be ruin, and he by

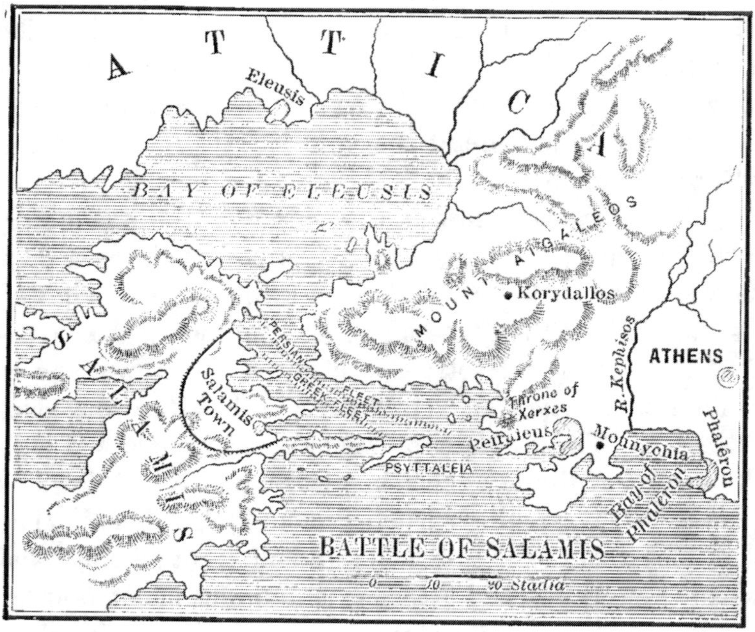

stratagem kept every ship in its place. He sent secret word to the Persians that the Greek fleet would soon be in full retreat, and the Persian admiral sent two hundred vessels to blockade the farther extremity of the strait, so that flight was impossible.

24. When everything was in readiness, Xerxes, from a throne built for him on the shore so that he might be a spectator of the fight, gave the signal to advance. At once all the long banks of oars in the thousand ships flashed in the light and dipped in the water. But here, as at Marathon, the way was narrow, and there was no

chance for the display of the full power of the Persian fleet. In a hand-to-hand conflict they stood no chance with the Greeks, and Xerxes, with despair in his heart, saw two hundred of his best ships sunk or captured and many more seriously disabled, while the Greeks had suffered little loss.

25. Themistocles remained all night at his anchorage, ready to renew the conflict on the morrow, but Xerxes, fearful for the fate of his bridge across the Hellespont, ordered the eight hundred remaining ships to sail for its protection, while he and his whole army marched as rapidly as possible for the same point. The number assembled to pass back into Asia was greatly diminished from the hosts which a few months before had so proudly marched to assured victory. Besides those lost in battle, thousands had perished through disease and famine. But the hope of final success was not entirely abandoned, and the Persian general, Mardonius, with three hundred thousand of the best soldiers of the invading army, were left to complete the conquest.

26. With the retreat of Xerxes, the Athenians returned to their city, finding their temples destroyed, and their homes desolated, but they immediately commenced the work of rebuilding, and, amid rejoicings and renewed hopes, the city arose from its ashes. The clash of arms gave place to the din of industry, and the fighting soldier was replaced by the peaceable citizen.

27. In the mean time, Mardonius went into winter quarters in the northern provinces, and during the winter he endeavored to effect by negotiation and bribery what he had failed to accomplish by arms. He succeeded in exciting the jealousy of several of the cities toward each other, so that it was difficult to bring about concert of action, and he succeeded in detaching Thebes entirely

from the confederacy, and arraying it against Athens. The Theban force which joined his army became one of the most formidable foes which the allied Greek had to meet.

28. The negotiations continued through the spring, but as summer approached the army of Mardonius was on the move. Sparta was not ready to meet the invader, and the Athenians once more took refuge on their ships, ten months after their return. Mardonius took possession of the city, and this time effectually destroyed it; but as nothing was to be gained by a further stay, he marched his army to Thebes, which became his headquarters. The Spartans were at length ready to march. They saw their city menaced, and their own safety demanded that the forces of Mardonius should be broken.

29. With the aid of their allies they put into the field an army, the largest that the Greeks ever mustered, variously reported as numbering one hundred thousand to one hundred and ten thousand men. These were under the command of the Spartan king, Pausanias. In September they set out for Thebes, and in a few days came up to the Persian army, which was stationed at Platæa, a short distance from Thebes. Here Mardonius had established a fortified camp to which he might retreat if defeated on the field. For eleven days the two armies confronted each other, neither anxious to strike the first blow. Then the supply of water for the Greek camp gave out, and Pausanias fell back to a better position.

30. This movement threw the Greek army into disorder, and the three main divisions became separated from one another. Perceiving this the next morning, Mardonius hastened with his Persians toward the higher ground, where the Spartan troops might be seen winding along under the hillside, for from the river-banks he could not

catch sight of the Athenians, who were hidden among the low hills which rose from the level plain.

31. The last momentous strife had now begun. It was the custom of the Spartans before beginning a battle to offer sacrifice, and to wait for an omen or sign from heaven on the offering. Even now, when the Persians had advanced to within bow-shot and were pouring flights of arrows upon the Spartans, Pausanias offered sacrifice. But the omens were bad, and forbade any action except in self defence. The Spartans knelt behind their shields, but the arrows pierced them, and the bravest men died sorrowfully, lamenting not for death, but because they died without striking a blow for Sparta. In his distress Pausanias called upon the goddess Hera, and the omens suddenly became favorable, and the Spartans with their Tegean allies threw themselves upon the enemy.

32. But the disparity of forces rendered the attack desperate. Fifty-three thousand Greeks in all were opposed to the overwhelming numbers of Mardonius. The Athenians were engaged elsewhere and could afford no assistance. The Persians had made a palisade of their wicker shields, behind which they could securely and effectually use their bows and arrows. By the first fierce onset of the Greeks this palisade went down, but the Asiatics, laying aside their bows, fought desperately with javelins and daggers. But they had no metal armor to defend them; and the Spartans, with their lances fixed and their shields touching each other, bore down everything before them.

33. The Persians fought with almost Hellenic heroism. Coming to close quarters, they seized the spears of their enemies and broke off their heads. Rushing forward singly or in small groups, they were borne down in the

crush and killed; still they were not dismayed; and the battle raged more fiercely on the spot where Mardonius, on his white horse, fought with the flower of his troops. At length Mardonius was slain, and when his chosen guards had fallen around him, the remainder of the Persians made their way to their fortified camp, and took refuge behind its wooden walls.

34. In the mean time the Athenian army had been confronted by the Persian-Theban allies. Here it was not a conflict between disciplined valor and barbaric hordes, but between Greek and Greek. The battle was long and bloody, but in the end the defenders of Greek liberty were victorious over those who would destroy it. The Theban force was not only defeated but annihilated, and then the Athenians hastened to the support of Pausanias. While the Spartans were the best-drilled soldiery in Greece for the field, they had little skill in siege operations, and the wooden walls of the Persian camp opposed to them an effective barrier.

35. While the Spartan force was engaged in abortive attempts, the Athenians and their allies came up fresh from their victory over the Thebans. Headed by the Tegeans, they burst like a deluge into the encampment, and the Persians, losing all heart, sought wildly to hide themselves like deer flying from lions. Then followed a carnage so fearful that out of two hundred and sixty thousand men not three thousand, it is said, remained alive.

36. Thus ended this formidable invasion, which threatened the very existence of Greece. The great wave of Oriental despotism had spent its force without submerging freedom. Thenceforth the wonderful Greek energy and creative power might be turned away from matters military and expended upon the arts of peace.

37. The Athenians returned to their city and found everything in ruins. Fire and hate had destroyed home and temple alike. All the accumulated wealth of generations was gone. Nothing was left but the indomitable energy which had been tested on so many trying emergencies, and the wonderful skill of eye and hand which came of inherited aptitude and long personal experience. Upon the old site a new city grew in a single generation, marvelous in its splendor of temple and palace, so light and airy, yet so strong and enduring, that after the lapse of twenty-five centuries the marble skeletons, though in ruins, stand, the admiration of all men and of all ages.

CHAPTER II.

CRUSADES AND THE CRUSADERS.

1. AFTER the destruction of Jerusalem by Titus, in the year 70 of the Christian era, Palestine continued for upward of two centuries in the condition of a Roman province, inhabited by a mixed population of pagans, Jews, and Christians. In Jerusalem, temples of Venus and Jupiter were erected on the most sacred spots of Christian history; and heathenism triumphed in the possession of the Holy City of two religions. On the establishment of Christianity in the Roman Empire by Constantine, in the year 321, this state of things was changed; Palestine and Jerusalem became objects of interest to all Christians, and crowds of pilgrims visited the localities celebrated by the evangelists. Splendid churches were erected on the ruins of pagan temples, and every spot pointed out as the scene of the memorable events in the life of Christ and his apostles was marked by a chapel or house of prayer. Jerusalem and the Holy Land became the resort of numerous bodies of clergy, who resided in the churches and monasteries which the piety of the wealthy had founded for them.

2. At the end of the fourth century, the gigantic Roman Empire was broken up into two, the Eastern, the capital of which was Constantinople, and the Western, the capital of which was Rome. It was to the former of

these that Syria and Palestine were attached. Before the end of the fifth century the Western Empire had been destroyed by the eruption of the German races, and the beginnings of a new European civilization were rising from its ruins. Meanwhile, the Eastern remained entire, till about the year 630, when the Arabs, burning with the spirit of conquest infused into them by the religion of Mohammed, poured into its provinces. Egypt, Syria, and Palestine were annexed as dependencies to the great Arabic Empire of the caliphs. The religion of Mohammed became dominant in the Holy Land, the temples and chapels were converted into mosques.

3. Numbers of pilgrims still continued each year to visit Palestine. In return for a certain tribute, the earlier caliphs permitted the Christians of Jerusalem to have a patriarch, and to carry on their own form of worship. Of all the caliphs, the celebrated Haroun al-Rashid, best known to us in the stories of the "Arabian Nights," was the most tolerant, and under him the Christians enjoyed perfect peace.

4. Great cruelties were practised by the Fatimite caliphs, who conquered Syria about the year 980. The pilgrims were robbed, beaten, and sometimes slain on their journey, the Christian residents oppressed by heavy impositions, and their feelings outraged by insults against their religion. These sufferings were slight, however, compared with those which they endured after the invasion and conquest of Palestine by the Turkish hordes in 1065. But recently converted to Moslemism, and therefore more rude and fanatical than the other Mohammedans, these Turks wreaked their vengeance on all alike—Christians, Jews, and even the native Mohammedans.

5. The news of the atrocities perpetrated by the Turks produced a deep sensation over the whole of Christen-

dom, as well among the Latin Christians as among the Greek Christians, the name given to the population of what remained of the old Byzantine Empire. The latter had reason to dread that, if the Turks were not checked, Constantinople, their capital, would soon share the same fate as Jerusalem. Accordingly, about the year 1073, the Greek Emperor, Manuel VII, sent to supplicate the assistance of the great Pope Gregory VII against the Turks. Till now there had prevailed a spirit of antagonism between the Greek and Latin churches, the former refusing to yield obedience to the pope of the West as the universal head of the Church. Gregory, therefore, eagerly received the application of the Greek Emperor, seeing the promise of the final subjection of the Greek to the Latin Church. He resolved to give the enterprise his countenance, and to march himself at the head of an army to rescue the Holy Sepulchre.

6. Gregory was prevented from ever carrying out his design, and the idea of a crusade gradually died away. Meanwhile, the Turks extended their victories at the expense of the Greek Empire. Before the accession of the celebrated Alexius Comnenus to the throne in 1081, the whole of Asia Minor was in the possession of the Turks, and broken up into a number of kingdoms, the sultans of which soon began to quarrel among themselves. The disturbed state of Asia Minor greatly increased the sufferings of the pilgrims; not one out of three returned to recount the story of his hardships.

7. Among those who undertook the pilgrimage to Jerusalem, when the dangers attending it were the greatest, was a native of Amiens in France, named Peter, who had become a monk and an ascetic, being called from his solitary manner of life, Peter the Hermit. He arrived safely at Jerusalem, and visited all the scenes sacred to a Chris-

tian's eyes. As he walked along the streets, looking at this and that holy spot, insolent and contemptuous Turks looked on and mocked him, and his spirit grew bitter within him, and his hand clutched itself convulsively as if longing for a sword.

8. Burning with a sense of injuries sustained by the Christians, and the desecration of the sacred places, he sought the counsel of Simeon, the Greek patriarch of Jerusalem. In reply to Peter's questions, he explained that nothing was to be expected from the Greek Empire in behalf of the Holy Land, the court of Constantinople was so dissolute and corrupt, and that the only hope was that the Latin princes might be persuaded to form a league for the grand purpose entertained by Gregory VII. "Write," Peter said to the patriarch, "to the pope and to all Latin Christians, and seal your letters with the signet of your office as patriarch of Jerusalem. As a penance for my sins, I will travel over Europe, I will describe everywhere the desolate condition of the Holy City, and exhort princes and people to wrest it from the profane hands of the infidels."

9. The letters were accordingly written, and the hermit set sail with them from Joppa. Arriving in Italy he presented the documents to the pope, Urban II, a pupil and *protégé* of Gregory VII, urging his holiness to use his authority, as the head of Christendom, to set in motion a scheme for regaining the birthplace of Christ. Enthusiasm is contagious, and the pope appears to have caught it instantly from one whose zeal was so unbounded. Giving the Hermit full powers, he sent him abroad to preach the holy war. Peter departed, going from town to town, and from village to village, and, in the language of the chroniclers, "traversing the whole of Europe in less than a year's time." His strange and wild aspect, his

St. Sophia, Constantinople.

glittering eye, his shrill and unearthly eloquence, the grandeur of his theme, his pathetic descriptions of Jerusalem and the Christians there, produced everywhere the most extraordinary sensations. "He set out," says a contemporary historian, "from whence I know not, nor with what purpose; but we saw him passing through the towns and villages, everywhere preaching, and the people flocking round him, loading him with gifts, and praising his sanctity with such eulogiums, that I never remember having seen so great honors paid to any other man. The people reverenced him so that they plucked the hairs from the mane of his mule, and kept them afterward as relics. Out of doors he generally wore a woolen tunic, with a brown mantle, which descended to his heels. His arms and feet were bare, he ate little or no bread, but lived on fish and wine."

10. Such being the success of the Hermit's mission, the pope showed his approbation of the project by summoning in the year 1095 two councils. The first of these was held at Placentia in March; ambassadors from the Greek Emperor appeared to petition for aid against the Turks, and the members of the council were unanimous in their support of the crusade. The second, the famous Council of Clermont, was held at the town of that name in Auvergne in the month of November. It was in the midst of an extremely cold winter, and the ground was covered with snow. During seven days the council sat with closed doors, while immense crowds from all parts of France flocked into the town, in the expectation that the pope himself would address the people.

11. All the neighborhood presented the appearance of a vast camp. Issuing from the church in his full canonicals, surrounded by his cardinals and bishops in all the splendor of ecclesiastical costume, the pope stood before

the populace on a high scaffolding, erected for the occasion, and covered with scarlet cloth. A brilliant array of bishops and cardinals surrounded him, and among them, humbler in rank but more important in the world's eye, the Hermit Peter, dressed in his simple woolen gown. The pope's eloquent words touched every heart. He was interrupted by the united voice of the people shouting "God wills it! God wills it!" Hushing the joyous tumult with a wave of his hand, the pontiff continued: "Be they then your war-cry in the combat, for those words came from God. Let the army of the Lord, when it rushes upon its enemies, shout but that one cry, 'God wills it! God wills it!' Let whoever is inclined to devote himself to this holy cause wear on his breast or back the sign of the holy cross." From this time the red cross was the sacred emblem of the crusaders.

THE FIRST CRUSADE.

12. Following the Council of Clermont, preparations for invading the Holy Land began in almost every country of Europe. The clanging of the smith's hammer, making or repairing armor, was heard in every village. All who had property of any description rushed to the mart to change it for hard cash. The nobles mortgaged their estates, the farmer endeavored to sell his plow, and the artisan his tools to purchase a sword for the deliverance of Jerusalem. Women disposed of their trinkets for the same purpose. During the spring and summer of 1096 the roads teemed with crusaders, all hastening to the towns and villages appointed as the rendezvous of the district. Very few knew where Jerusalem was. Some thought it fifty thousand miles away, and others imagined it but a month's journey; while at the sight of every tower

or castle the children exclaimed "Is that Jerusalem?" Little attempt at any organization was made, though the multitude had three leaders. It is said that the first band, consisting of twenty thousand foot, with only eight horsemen, were led by a Burgundian gentleman, called Walter the Penniless. They were followed by a rabble of forty thousand men, women, and children, led by Peter the Hermit, a medley of all nations and languages. Next followed a band of fifteen thousand men, mostly Germans, under a priest named Gottschalk. These three multitudes led the way in the crusades, pursuing the same route, that, namely, which leads through Hungary and Bulgaria toward Asia Minor.

13. Like their nominal leader, each of the followers of Walter the Penniless was poor to penury, and trusted for subsistence to the chances of the road. In Hungary they met with loud resistance from the people, whose houses they attacked and plundered, but in Bulgaria the natives declared war against the hungry horde; they were dispersed and almost exterminated. Some of the survivors retraced their steps; the rest, among whom was Walter, reached Constantinople, where they awaited the arrival of Peter and his companions. The Hermit, who had the same difficulties to contend with in marching through Hungary and Bulgaria, reached Constantinople with his army greatly reduced, and in a most deplorable condition. Here he and Walter joined forces, the Hermit assuming the superior command. They were hospitably received by the emperor, but their riotous conduct soon wearied out his patience, and he was glad to listen to a proposal of the Hermit to furnish them with the means of passing at once into Asia. The rabble accordingly crossed the Bosphorus, and took up their quarters in Bethynia. Here they became perfectly ungovern-

able, ravaging the country around, and committing incredible excesses; at length Peter, utterly disgusted and despairing, left them to their own guidance and returned to Constantinople. The bravest of them were annihilated in a battle fought near Nice, Walter the Penniless falling with seven mortal wounds. Between two and three thousand alone escaped, brought back to Constantinople by the troops of Alexius, who rescued them from the Turks. The emperor dismissed them, with orders to return home, and thus ended the disastrous expedition of Walter the Penniless and Peter the Hermit.

14. The fifteen thousand Germans led by Gottschalk never reached Constantinople, being slaughtered or dispersed during their passage through Hungary. Hungary was also fatal to another army of crusaders, the fourth in order, but greatly exceeding in numbers the other three put together. This terrible horde, consisting of about two hundred thousand, swept through Germany committing horrible outrages, especially against the Jews, whom they murdered without mercy. They were preceded by a goose and a goat, to which they attributed divine powers. As the rabble advanced, the Hungarians gave themselves up for lost, the king and nobles were preparing to flee, when the mass fell asunder of its own accord. Many were slain by the enraged Hungarians. Some escaped to the north, a few ultimately joined the succeeding bands of crusaders, but the majority perished. Thus, within a few months, upward of a quarter of a million of human beings were swept out of existence. And they had spent their lives, without one important result having been accomplished, without one glorious feat having been achieved.

15. This was the worst paroxysm of the madness of Europe, and this passed, her chivalry stepped upon the

scene. Men of cool heads, mature plans, and invincible courage stood forward to lead and direct, not mere fanatical masses, but the gentry, yeomanry, and serfs of feudal Europe. These were the true crusaders. Altogether they formed six armies, marching separately, and at considerable intervals of time. First came the army of Godfrey of Bouillon, Duke of Lorraine, the pride of his age for all noble and knightly virtues, immortalized by the poet Tasso. He had risen from a sick-bed to join the crusade, and sold his lordship to raise the necessary money; around his standard assembled many of the best knights of the age. In the month of August, 1096, they commenced their march, through Hungary and Bulgaria.

16. Four other chiefs of the royal blood of Europe also assumed the cross, and led each his army to the Holy Land; Hugh, Count of Vermandois, brother of the king of France; Robert, Duke of Normandy, the elder brother of William Rufus; Robert, Count of Flanders, and Bohemond, Prince of Tarentum, eldest son of the celebrated Robert Guiscard. With Bohemond, and second in command in the army, came Tancred, the favorite hero of all the historians of the crusade, so young, so valiant, so enthusiastic. There was not among them all, says Tasso, a greater warrior, nor any one of more courteous behavior, of fairer countenance, or of loftier and more intrepid heart. The last army was led by the haughty and resolute Count Raimond of Toulouse.

17. To detail the progress of the various armies is unnecessary. Upward of six hundred thousand warriors of the West, beside a multitude of priests, women, and children, were at last actually encamped on Asiatic soil. It was literally a moving nation, in which all languages were spoken, all costumes worn. There was the fair-haired son of the north, with broad, open forehead, mild blue

eyes, sanguine complexion, and large frame; there the dark visaged southron, with his flashing glance and fiery soul; there was the knight in his armor, the priest in his robes, the foot-soldier in his tough jerkin, the unkempt serf with his belt of rope. There were pawing horses, swearing grooms, carts full of provisions, sacks, groups of gossiping women, crowds of merry children. Under the bright sun of Asia, all was gaudy and brilliant. Spear-points glittered, breast-plates and helmets gleamed, thousands of targets displayed their painted glories, pennons of blue, purple, and white streamed from every tent, while heavier flags flapped their sullen folds; and everywhere, on shield, flag, helmet, tunic, and coat of mail, was seen blazoned the holy sign of the red cross. Walking through all these, heedless of the looks cast upon him, and hearing not the oft-repeated bugle-blasts from all parts of the camp, might be seen a man of small stature, thin and poorly clad, with down-cast face, wild, unsettled eye, and timid, nervous gait. It was the man who had created it all—Peter the Hermit. He had crossed from Constantinople with Godfrey of Bouillon. His revenge was near! On, on, then, to the Holy City!

18. Alas, the Holy City was yet far distant! Not much more than half their journey in point of space had been accomplished, and in point of difficulty and peril their march had little more than begun, for they had just entered the countries of the infidels. Months had to roll on, and many battles to be fought, ere the pinnacles of the Holy City should greet their longing eyes.

19. The route of the crusading armies lay in a south-easterly direction, through Asia Minor, and then southward to Jerusalem, along the shores of the Levant. Their march along this route, counting from the time of their crossing into Asia Minor, May, 1097, to the time when

they came in sight of Jerusalem and laid siege to it, June, 1099, occupied upward of two years. Countless were the dangers to which the crusaders were subject in this trial. Of the many sieges two are especially memorable, that of Nice and that of Antioch.

20. The siege of Nice was the first exploit in which the crusading armies were engaged. During these six weeks the slaughter of the Christians, by the arrows of the Turkish garrison, and by the bolts and large stones which they discharged from mangonels and catapults, was immense. The city surrendered at last, not, however, to the Latin chiefs, but to an envoy of the Greek Emperor Alexius, who contrived to enter into communication with the besieged and induced them to capitulate. Angry and dissatisfied, the crusaders left their encampment and resumed their march, not in one mass, but in several bodies. At length the scattered armies reunited for the siege of Antioch toward the end of October, 1097. All the known means of attack were put in operation; movable towers were constructed from which to discharge missiles into the city. The walls were battered, and the sallies of the besieged bravely met, still without any effective result. At the end of ten days famine stared them in the face, so extravagant were they in the use of their stores. Pestilence joined its ravages, and instead of the brave army of chivalry which had sat down before Antioch, was to be seen a crowd of gaunt and famishing creatures, with scarcely a thought but that of procuring food. Multitudes died, desertions became numerous.

21. The chiefs began to weary of the expedition, and, most disgraceful of all, Peter the Hermit turned his back on the enterprise, and had actually fled several miles on his way home, when he was brought back by the soldiers of Tancred and forced to undergo a public repri-

mand. At length, after infinite sufferings on the part of Antioch was taken on the 3d of June, 1098, by means of the treachery of an Armenian captain, whom the Turks had intrusted with the command of one of the towers, and who admitted a number of the crusaders during a dark and stormy night.

22. Imagination can not conceive a scene more dreadful than that presented by the devoted city of Antioch on that night of horror. The crusaders fought with a blind fury which fanaticism and suffering alike incited. No quarter was shown. At daylight the massacre ceased, and the crusaders gave themselves up to plunder. They found gold, jewels, and rich fabrics in abundance, but of provisions little of any kind. Suddenly they were roused from their sloth and pleasure by the appearance before Antioch of an immense army, which the Persian caliph had dispatched to sweep the Christian locusts from the face of the earth. Great was the alarm of the Christians when they saw this splendid host of more than two hundred thousand men encamped around the hills of Antioch. The corn and wine found in the city were soon exhausted; all the horrors of a second famine began.

23. Many deserted and escaped over the walls, carrying the news of the sad condition of the Christians back toward Europe. The worst consequence of these desertions was, that the Greek Emperor Alexius, who, hearing of the successes of the Latins, was on his march to assist the crusaders, was deterred from advancing, and returned to Constantinople. With increasing famine came a pestilence, so that in a short time but sixty thousand remained of the three hundred thousand that had invested Antioch. But this bitter extremity knit the leaders more firmly together, and Bohemond, Godfrey, and Tancred swore never to desert the cause while life lasted.

24. It is said that belief in the remarkable fulfillment of a dream brought hope once more to the disheartened crusaders. Peter Barthelmy, a priest of Provence, dreamed, he said, that Saint Andrew appeared to him in the night, and informed him that underneath a certain spot in the floor of the church of Saint Peter was buried the identical lance with which the Roman soldiers pierced the side of Christ as he hung on the cross. This relic, said the apparition, was to be the guarantee of God's presence and their guide to victory. Twelve persons were chosen to conduct the search. A whole day was spent in vain, the workmen were tired out, and still no lance was found. At last Peter descended into the pit and began to dig the loose earth. Suddenly a cry of joy was heard, and stretching himself to his full height, Peter handed up into the eager fingers of those above an actual rusty lance-head. In an instant it was noised abroad that the holy relic had been found. What remained now but to issue forth and discomfit the infidel host.

25. The infidel host was discomfited. On the 28th of June, 1098, two hundred thousand Turks, in the full flush of health and strength, were routed, outside the walls of Antioch, by a half-famished Christian army. Antioch was bestowed upon Bohemond, and it was resolved that the army should remain there to recruit before advancing toward Jerusalem. The tragical fate of Peter Barthelmy must be mentioned. Many of the crusaders had begun to question the genuineness of the relic he had found. He was prevailed upon to submit to the ordeal of fire, and perished in the flames. From that moment the story of the relic lost credit.

26. It was on a lovely morning in the summer of 1099 that the forty thousand crusaders, who were all that remained of the vast army which had two years ago

laid seige to Nice, were recompensed for all their toils by a sight of the Holy City, bathed in the splendor of eastern sunshine. The name "Jerusalem" escaped from every lip; some leaped and shouted, some kneeled and prayed, some wept, some threw themselves prostrate and kissed the earth, some gazed and trembled. "All had much ado," says the quaint Fuller, "to manage so much gladness."

27. Preparations for a siege were soon under way. The besiegers, who had gained skill by their former attempts, employed all the methods of attack that experience could suggest or courage execute, while the garrison of forty thousand Turks, who maintained the city for their master, the caliph of Egypt, resisted with determined obstinacy. At length, after a confession of sins by the whole army, and a penitential procession around the walls, a simultaneous attack was made with battering-rams, mangonels, and all manner of besieging engines. At one quarter a huge wooden tower was wheeled close to the walls, a movable bridge was let down, and, bounding across it, a soldier named Lutold was the first man to stand upon the battlements. Godfrey of Bouillon and a number of knights sprang after him, and the Christians were within Jerusalem. Meanwhile, at another part of the wall, Tancred and Robert of Normandy had shattered open a gate, and rushed in with their men; while at a third part of the city, Raimond of Toulouse effected an entrance for himself and his followers by the help of scaling-ladders. In an instant after, the banner of the cross floated upon the walls of Jerusalem. The crusaders, raising once more their redoubtable war-cry, rushed on from every side, and the city was taken. The battle raged for several hours, and the Christians gave no quarter. Peter the Hermit, who had remained so long under the veil of neglect, was

repaid that day for all his zeal and all his suffering. He was once more the idol of the army, but history is silent concerning the remainder of his life.

28. Eight days after the capture of the city, the Latin chiefs unanimously elected Godfrey of Bouillon king of Jerusalem. A new Christian state was thus founded in Syria, consisting at first of little more than the mere city of Jerusalem, but extending by subsequent battles and conquests until it included the whole of Palestine. A language resembling Norman-French was established in this kingdom, and a code of feudal laws drawn up for its government. The clergy also obtained their share of the conquest, Jerusalem was created into a patriarchate, and Bethlehem into a bishopric. The foundation of the Latin Kingdom of Jerusalem in July, 1099, was the consummation of the first crusade.

29. A period of fifty years succeeded, during which time many battles were fought with the Saracens of Syria and Egypt, the result of which was to strengthen the Latin state. No fewer than five hundred thousand persons set out from Europe for Syria, incited by the news of the success of the first crusade. The three centers from which the Christian power sought to spread itself through the Mussulman possessions were Jerusalem, Antioch, and Edessa.

30. The very spirit of the crusade seemed to have died out. The Latin Kingdom of Jerusalem had become, like any other kingdom of the period, a country in which men built houses, plowed land, made bargains, gave feasts, etc., drank, laughed, talked, quarreled, and went to law. The fall of Edessa, the first conspicuous success of the Turks, came like a surprise upon the Latin population of Syria. An attempt was made by the Christians to recover the city, but it failed, and the frontier of Syria was open to invasion from the East.

THE SECOND CRUSADE.

31. The fall of Edessa, and the petitions of the people of Palestine for aid, produced a sensation throughout Europe, and especially in France. Nor was an apostle wanting worthy to fill the place of Peter, and to summon the chivalry of Europe to a second crusade. Commissioned by Pope Eugenius for that purpose, the famous Saint Bernard, Abbot of Clairvaux in Champagne, traveled through France and Germany, exerting the power of his marvelous eloquence in recruiting the armies of the cross. The chiefs of the second crusade were two of the most powerful princes of Europe, Louis VII, King of France, and Conrad III, Emperor of Germany. Under their command upward of one million two hundred thousand men, collected from all parts of Europe, marched toward Palestine in two great armies, early in 1147.

32. Notwithstanding the vastness of the preparations, the expedition was a total failure. The events of the last fifty years had rendered the policy of the Greek princes hostile to the crusades. Manuel Comnenus, the grandson of Alexius, who now occupied the throne, suffered both armies to pass into Asia Minor, where, misled by Greek scouts, the army of Conrad was all but destroyed by the Turks, near Iconium, while the army of Louis, after undergoing infinite hardships, was wrecked in the defiles of the Pisidian mountains. The fragments of the two armies uniting made their way to Syria, where they cooperated with forces of the princes of Jerusalem and Antioch, in laying seige to Damascus, but without effect. In 1149 Conrad and Louis returned to Europe, and the second crusade was at an end, having attained nothing but the expenditure of more than a million of lives.

THE THIRD CRUSADE.

33. A period of forty years elapsed before Europe fitted out another crusade. Meanwhile the struggle between the Christian and the Turks in Syria was carried on without intermission. Noureddin, the son of the conqueror of Edessa, displayed a genius which astonished both Christians and Turks. Keeping possession of Edessa, he aimed at extending his conquest at the expense of the Christians still further. For some time he was kept in check by the abilities of Baldwin III, King of Jerusalem. On his death, in 1162, his brother Amalric, far inferior to Baldwin in ability, succeeded to the throne.

34. At this crisis, while Noureddin, the Sultan of Aleppo, and Amalric, the Christian King of Jerusalem, were the rival powers in Syria, occurred a circumstance which exercised considerable influence on the subsequent course of events, and which makes necessary a retrospective glance.

35. At the time of the first crusade Palestine was the scene of a violent contest between the Turks, who had poured down from the North, conquering as they went, and the Fatimites of Egypt, who had possessed Syria for nearly a century. The Turks had at first been irresistible. The Fatimites, however, had been able to recover Jerusalem from the hands of their enemies, and held it when besieged by the Christians. Interrupted in their conflict with each other for the sovereignty of Palestine, the Fatimites and Turks turned their arms with one accord against the invader. In the person of Noureddin the Turkish power was now increasing. The Fatimite dynasty of Egypt, meanwhile, had long been showing signs of decay, the caliphs having become mere tools in the hands of their viziers. In 1163 one of these viziers, Shawer, finding

himself expelled from his post by a rival, sought refuge at the court of Aleppo, and applied to the sultan for assistance. Noureddin eagerly embraced an opportunity for obtaining a footing in Egypt, and sent two persons, Chyrkouh and his nephew Saladin, to displace the usurping vizier and re-establish Shawer. They, however, usurped the government, and Shawer applied to the King of Jerusalem, Amalric, for assistance. Amalric in turn attempted usurpation, and again the officers of Noureddin came to the aid of Shawer. The vizier paid the penalty of his fickleness by losing his head, and his post was occupied by Chyrkouh, who, while ruling Egypt as a vizier of the Fatimite caliph, was in reality the lieutenant of Noureddin.

36. On the death of Chyrkouh, Saladin was appointed to the viziership. The caliph fancied that he would now regain the control of his own dominions, but he little knew the character of his new vizier. Saladin soon effected a revolution in Egypt, declared the Fatimite dynasty to be at an end, and subjected the country once more to the nominal authority of the Bagdad caliphs, whom Noureddin professed to reverence as the supreme heads of the Mohammedan Empire. Nor did he stop here. He soon showed a disposition to shake off the supremacy of Noureddin, and the sultan of Aleppo was marching into Egypt to vindicate his authority, when he suddenly died in the year 1171.

37. Saladin now saw the great obstacle to his ambition removed, and began to aim at realizing those schemes of sovereignty which Noureddin had projected. The state of the Christian kingdom during the ten or twelve years which followed directly favored his plans. Civil dissensions arose which the keen eye of Saladin discovered, and, already master of all Syria, he resolved to complete his

greatness by the conquest of Palestine. Accordingly, when in the year 1187 it was known that he was on his march against Jerusalem, the Christian crusaders saw the necessity of abandoning their dissensions and uniting cordially against the invader. Town after town surrendered to the victorious Saracen, and, in October, 1187, Jerusalem itself, after fourteen days' defense, was obliged to submit to his mercy. The conduct of Saladin on this occasion was more generous than might have been expected. A moderate ransom was fixed for every individual, on the payment of which he was at liberty to remove with his goods to whatever place he chose. To the Christian ladies, Saladin's conduct was courteous in the extreme, so that it became a remark among the Latins of Palestine that Saladin was a barbarian only in name.

38. Thus, after ninety years, was the Holy City again inhabited by the infidel, and all the fruits of the first crusade lost, as it seemed to the world. Saladin now possessed the whole of Palestine, with the single exception of the city of Tyre, which was gallantly defended by Conrad, Marquis of Montferrat.

39. The epidemic frenzy which had been gradually cooling was now extinct, or nearly so, and the nations of Europe looked with cold indifference upon the armaments of their princes. But chivalry was now in all its glory, and it continued to supply armies for the Holy Land. Poetry more than religion inspired the Third Crusade. The knights and their retainers listened with delight to the martial and amatory strains of the ministrels, minnesingers, and troubadors. Men fought not so much for the holy sepulchre as to gain glory for themselves in the best and only field where glory could be obtained. They fought not as zealots, but as soldiers, not for religion, but for honor.

40. The first to take the field was the illustrious German emperor, Frederick Barbarossa. Marching from Ratisbon at the head of a magnificent army in 1189, he fought his way through the Greek dominions, advanced through Asia Minor, conquering as he went, and was already on the borders of Palestine, when, imprudently bathing, he was cut off in the seventieth year of his age. His army suffered greatly from the difficulties of their march and the attacks of the Saracens. The wrecks of it under Frederick's son, the Duke of Swabia, proved a most valuable reinforcement to the Christians in Syria, who had by this time rallied and combined against the domination of Saladin, laying siege to the city of Acre on the sea-coast, a town of so much importance that the possession of it was considered almost equivalent to being master of the whole country.

41. Upon this siege, commenced in August, 1189, was concentrated all the force at the command of the Christians in Palestine, the remnants of the two great military orders the Knights Templars and the Knights Hospitallers, the survivors of Frederick's army, together with such bodies of crusaders as were continually arriving from Europe by sea. Guy de Lusignan was the commander of the besieging forces, and so skillfully was his army fortified that Saladin was unable to dislodge him. For two-and-twenty months the siege continued, and many engagements had taken place between the Christian army and that of Saladin, which occupied the mountains to the south, but without visible advantage on either side.

42. Such was the position of affairs when, early in the summer of 1191, Philip, of France, and Richard Cœur de Lion, of England, arrived with their fleets. The struggle was soon over, and on the 12th of July, 1191, Acre surrendered to the Christians. Had the crusaders

been united among themselves, the fall of this city might have been but preliminary to the recovery of the whole country. The rivalry of the kings of France and England, however, prevented their cordial co-operation, and, not long after the capture of Acre, Philip ruined the cause of the crusade by returning to Europe.

43. After gaining many important successes against Saladin, and earning for himself the reputation of the most valiant knight of the age, Richard, involved in disputes with the other chiefs of the crusade, and anxious to revisit England, where his presence was becoming daily more necessary, was glad to conclude an honorable peace. Saladin, on his part, was equally willing to end a struggle which had cost him so much. A truce was concluded for three years and eight months, during which Christian pilgrims were to enjoy the liberty of visiting Jerusalem without hindrance.

44. Saladin entertained many Christians in his own palace, from which they returned, their tongues laden with praises of the noble infidel. Richard and Saladin never met, but each admired the prowess and nobleness of soul of his rival.

45. The Christians and Moslems no longer looked upon each other as barbarians, to whom mercy was a crime. Each host entertained the highest admiration for the bravery and magnanimity of the other, and in their occasional truces met upon the most friendly terms. When Richard, the lion-hearted king of England, lay in his tent consumed by a fever, there came into the camp camels laden with snow, sent by his enemy, the Sultan Saladin, to assuage his disease, the homage of one brave soldier to another. But, when Richard was returning to England, it was by a Christian prince that he was treacherously seized and secretly confined.

46. It was on the 25th of October, 1192, that Richard set sail for Europe. Forced by stress of weather to land at Zara, he made the attempt to journey through the continent, and was arrested and held a prisoner while passing through the dominions of his enemy and former fellow-crusader, the archduke of Austria, and remained in prison in Vienna for several months. He returned to England in 1194, and died in 1199. His great antagonist, Saladin, had died in 1193, not long after the Christian armies left Palestine. At the end of the crusade, the Crescent waved as defiantly as ever over the land of Israel.

THE FOURTH CRUSADE.

47. The fourth crusade, from 1195 to 1198, led by Henry VI of Germany, was equally a failure. There were gained some brilliant victories, but dissensions divided the armies, and at last a truce was made with the Mohammedans. It is true that these victories made the crusaders masters of the sea-coast, but, when the armies departed, the Christian king found himself in possession of cities which he was unable to garrison, and which he felt would be held only by the sufferance of the enemy.

THE FIFTH CRUSADE.

48. In the year 1203 a new crusade was set on foot, commanded by several of the most powerful nobles of Italy and France. Instead of marching at once against the infidels, the crusaders suffered themselves to be drawn into a contest with the Greek empire. Just at this time the emperor of the Greeks had been deposed and deprived of his eyes by his own brother. His son, Alexius, fled to Europe, and petitioned the assistance of the Latin

princes against the usurper, promising in return to use his efforts to bring about a union of the Greek with the Latin church, and to employ all the resources of his kingdom against the infidels of Syria. The temptation of such a prospect could not be resisted; the crusaders marched into Greece, laid siege to Constantinople, and took the city by storm A. D. 1204, thereby establishing Latin Christianity in the eastern metropolis,but at what a cost. Neither the works of God nor man were respected by the invaders; they vented their brutal ferocity upon the one, and satisfied their avarice upon the other. "In St. Sophia, the silver was stripped from the pulpit, an exquisite and highly-prized table of oblation was broken in pieces, the sacred chalices were turned into drinking-cups, the gold fringe was ripped off the veil of the sanctuary. Asses and horses were led into the churches to carry off the spoil.

49. "Many beautiful bronze pieces, above all price as works of art, were broken into pieces to be sold as old metal. The finely chiseled marble was also destroyed by the same spirit of vandalism. Two thousand people were put to the sword; had there been less plunder, the slaughter would in all probability have been much greater."

50. For fifty years the empire was ruled over by the Franks. Meanwhile the knights, plunged in the luxury of the city, heeded not the appeals from Palestine, but allowed the besieged and suffering, for whose rescue they had enlisted, to linger and die without an effort on their behalf. Moved to desperation, in this emergency, the Christians sent to Europe a heart-rending cry for help.

THE SIXTH CRUSADE.

51. The urgent appeal from Palestine caused Pope Innocent III to earnestly preach a new crusade, and he

crowned his labors and appeals with his famous exclamation, "Sword, sword, start from thy scabbard, and sharpen thyself to kill." Though the many disastrous and fruitless expeditions had so dampened the ardor of men that they gave little heed to his appeals, the zeal of the young was kindled for the cause to which their elders seemed so indifferent.

52. The children of Germany and France caught the madness of the hour, and resolved upon a crusade of their own. Inspired by the preaching of a fanatical priest named Nicholas, twenty thousand boys of the average age of twelve years assembled at Cologne. They came from all ranks of life, and the heir of the proud noble marched side by side with the son of the humblest peasant. Sisters, priests, and servants joined the throng, swelling the numbers and adding to the confusion.

53. Their journey began in July, 1212, and their destination was Palestine, and they were to go by way of Rome, so as to obtain the assistance and the blessing of the Pope. In their ignorance these poor children thought that Palestine was but a few miles distant, and before the close of the first day's march excited voices were heard asking if the holy sepulchre was in sight. Slowly onward the multitude moved up the Rhine, and over the Mont Cenis pass of the Alps, into Italy.

54. But day by day hearts became sick with continued disappointment, and little feet weary with the never-ending miles which stretched before. The weak and the sickly were the first to give out, and, though they struggled to keep their places in the ranks, one by one they fell by the wayside to die alone, with no loving hands to soothe their last moments or to moisten their parched lips with a drop of cold water. The path of the youthful crusaders might be traced by the marks left by thou-

sands of bleeding feet and by the victims stretched in death along the course.

55. Death, disease, and desertion soon thinned their ranks to such an extent that only one half of their original number lived to reach the summit of the Alps and look down into Italy. The journey across the mountains was a fearful one. They had left home in summer, when their raiment was thin; it had become scanty and ragged in the long and dusty march, so that they were exposed to the full severity of the cold. The rocks cut their shoeless feet, but nothing remained but to press onward or to lie down and die.

56. Only seven thousand lived to reach Genoa, where they were received coldly, but where they were at last permitted to stay a week to rest. Then again onward through the plains of Italy, until all that survived made their way to Rome. Pope Innocent partook of the fanaticism which affected all Europe, but the sight of these little victims of the universal delusion, reduced to mere spectres by hardships, disease, and famine, aroused in him an unexpected human sympathy. He blessed the children, forbade them to go farther, and when rested sent them back to their German homes.

57. The winter had passed and the spring had come again before the few survivors reached their beloved fatherland. Day by day there came straggling into the German cities groups of these victims, their heads drooping for shame, their eyes red with tears, their clothing in rags. Many died upon realizing the last hope which had sustained them so long. Sad-eyed mothers looked in vain among the thin ranks for their beloved ones, and time only soothed the untold misery of this wild enterprise.

58. Soon after the departure of the German children on their crusade under Nicholas, another of about equal

numbers set out from Cologne by a different route. They crossed the Alps by the pass of St. Gothard, and descended into Eastern Italy. Keeping along the coast of the Adriatic, they at last came to the southern front of the peninsula, and could go no farther. They met with a fate similar to that of the first band, with the additional horror that many of them were seized by Turkish pirates and carried away into life-long slavery. The few who survived to reach Southern Italy embarked on a vessel, and never were heard of more. No messenger even returned to the vine-clad hills of the Rhine to report the fate of the little ones, and they all disappeared from the aching gaze of anxious mothers as though the earth had swallowed them up.

59. The third children's crusade set out from France under the leadership of a bare-footed friar named Stephen. They numbered thirty thousand, and their first destination was Marseilles, whence they were to take shipping for Palestine through means directly provided by the Lord. Through the broad fields of France, during the hot summer days, the crusaders marched, every mile marked by victims; and, when the white walls of the city of their destination became visible, their numbers were reduced one half.

60. The charity of Marseilles was taxed to its utmost to provide for the fifteen thousand mouths open to receive it. Through weary weeks the children waited in vain for the promised aid from the Lord. Despair was more fatal than famine, and soon two thirds of those who had reached the city perished. When their numbers were reduced to five thousand, apparently the promise of Divine aid was fulfilled. Two wealthy and benevolent merchants volunteered to send the children on to their destination. Seven ships were prepared, and into these

the five thousand crowded, believing their troubles were at an end.

61. The ships sailed out of port, freighted with mother love and religious blessings. To anxious eyes that watched their departure, their white sails, lessening in the distance, wafted back messages of hope and assurance. At the dawn of another day the last speck had disappeared, and the blue waves of the Mediterranean rolled tranquilly, as if jealously guarding the secrets of fate. But time went on. Homeward-bound vessels, direct from the scene of conflict, saw the precious fleet. News of stern conflicts with the infidels was brought by wandering palmers; but from sailor merchant, from peasant warrior, and from noble scarred with Saracenic wounds, there was a death-like silence in regard to the little wanderers. Streaming eyes fixed upon the East looked in vain until all tears were quenched in death.

62. Eighteen years passed since the children's fleet sailed out of European life. Then a vague rumor of treachery began to circulate, and, little by little, the details came out of one of the most inhuman crimes that ever shocked the hearts of men. The benevolent merchants who furnished the ships had sold the children to the barbarous Moslems, and the course of the fleet was turned from east to south. On the second day out a great storm arose, and two of the ships foundered, and all on board perished. A more horrible fate awaited the survivors. Landing in a city of the Moors in northern Africa, they were conducted to a secure prison, and from the gloomy portals they passed out into distant and perpetual slavery. One by one the captives died, some by disease, some by cruelty, others passed away in old age. At length all dropped their weary burdens, and their toils and sorrows ended. Not one of the hundreds that sailed

out of Marseilles on that sunny afternoon ever saw Europe again. Rarely in the history of the world has a story in real life been freighted with so much woe as fell to the lot of the victims of the strange madness which swept over Europe less than seven hundred years ago. Peace to their memories!

63. At last an army was organized, and Innocent announced that he himself would lead the host to the defense of the holy sepulchre; but his death intervened before the project was ripe. Andrew, king of Hungary, was the only monarch who had leisure or inclination to leave his dominions. He led the army to Palestine and defeated the Saracens, but failed to follow up his victory, and soon after abandoned the enterprise. The Duke of Austria, who succeeded him as leader, directed the whole energy of the crusade against Egypt; and Damietta, which commanded the river Nile, was chosen as the first point of attack. Finding themselves unable to successfully defend the city, the Moslems offered to yield the whole of Palestine to the Christians upon the condition of the evacuation of Egypt. With a blindness almost incredible these terms were refused, and a last attack made on the walls of Damietta. The besieged made but slight resistance, and the Christians entered the city, to find out of seventy thousand but three thousand remaining, so fearful had been the scourge of plague and famine. Several months were spent in Damietta. The climate either weakened the frames or obscured the understandings of the Christians, for after their conquest they remained inactive until the Moslems recuperated their army and were able to recapture Damietta and expel the Crusaders from Egypt.

64. With a view to the recovery of the Holy Land, Frederick II, of Germany, had been married to Iolante, the heiress of the kingdom of Jerusalem. His early

life was spent in Sicily, in familiar intercourse with Jews and Arabs, and Sicily was to the last the favored portion of his dominion. The emperor's court was given up to unpardonable frivolities in the eyes of Pope Gregory IX, one of whose first pontifical acts was to summon Frederick to a new crusade. The emperor paid little heed to the aged Pope's exhortations and commands, postponing from time to time the period of his departure. He embarked at last, but in ten days returned. The Pope was not to be trifled with, and pronounced his excommunication. Frederick treated it with contempt, and appealed to Christendom to sustain him. For this he underwent a more tremendous excommunication, but his partisans in Rome raised an insurrection and expelled the Pope.

65. And now Frederick set sail of his own accord on his crusading expedition. On reaching the Holy Land he was received with joy by the knights and pilgrims, but the clergy held aloof from him as under the ban of the Church. He negotiated privately with the Sultan of Egypt. The Christian camp was thronged with Saracens. The emperor wore a Saracen dress. In his privacy he did not hesitate to say, "I came not here to deliver the Holy City, but to maintain my estimation among the Franks." To the Sultan he appealed: "Out of your goodness surrender to me Jerusalem as it is, that I may be able to lift up my head among the kings of Christendom." Accordingly, the city was surrendered to him. The Pope repudiated the transaction.

66. While the emperor proclaimed his successes to Europe, the pope denounced them. Frederick crowned himself at Jerusalem, being unable to find any ecclesiastic who dared to perform the ceremony, and departed from the Holy Land. He prepared to enter on his conflict with

the pontiff, and drew over to his side the general sentiment of Europe; the Pope was made to give way, and peace proclaimed. The treaty, which closed the sixth crusade, was for ten years.

THE SEVENTH CRUSADE.

67. On neither side probably was the truce strictly kept, and the injuries done to pilgrims on their way from Acre to Jerusalem were alleged as a sufficient reason for sending out the expedition headed by Richard, Earl of Cornwall, brother of the English Henry III, and afterward King of the Romans. This expedition may be regarded as the seventh in the list of crusades, and deserves notice as having been brought to an end, like that of Frederick, by a treaty, in 1240. The terms of the latter covenant were even more favorable to the Christians, but, two years later, the Latin power, such as it was, was swept away by the sword of Korasmians, pushed onward by the hordes of Jenghiz Khan. The awful inroad was alleged by Pope Innocent IV as reason for summoning Christendom again to the rescue of the Holy Land.

THE EIGHTH CRUSADE.

68. Nearly seven years passed away before the French king, Louis IX, was able to set sail for Egypt. The royal saint, who lives for us in the quaint and graphic account of his seneschal Joinville, may with truth be said to have been animated by a spirit of devotion and self-sacrifice. Intolerant in theory and bigoted in language, Louis had that true charity which would make him succor his enemies not less than his friends. Nor was his bravery less signal than his gentleness. His dauntless courage saved

his army from complete destruction at Mansourah in 1249, but his offer to exchange Damietta for Jerusalem was rejected, and in the retreat, during which they were compelled to fight at desperate disadvantage, Louis was taken prisoner. With serene patience he underwent suffering, for which the Saracens, so Joinville tells us, frankly confessed that they would have renounced Mahommed; and, when the payment of his ransom set him free, he made a pilgrimage in sackcloth to Nazareth in 1250. As a general he achieved nothing, but his humiliation involved no dishonor; and the genuineness of his faith, his devotion, and his love had been fully tested in the furnace of affliction.

69. The crusading fire was now rapidly burning itself out. In the West there was nothing to awaken again the enthusiasm which had been stirred by Peter the Hermit and St. Bernard, while in Palestine itself the only signs of genuine activity were furnished by the antagonism between the religious orders there. The quarrels of Templars and Hospitallers led to a pitched battle in 1259, in which almost all the Templars were slain.

THE NINTH CRUSADE.

70. Some eight years later the tidings that Antioch had been taken by the infidels revived in St. Louis the old yearning for the rescue of the holy places. Cheered by the sympathy of Pope Clement IV, he embarked with an army of sixty thousand in 1270, but a storm drove his ships to Sardinia, and thence they sailed for Tunis. They encamped on the site of Carthage, when a plague broke out. The saintly king was among the victims, and the truest of all crusaders died. In the following year Edward, of England, reached Acre, took Nazareth—the in-

habitants of which he massacred—fell sick, and during his sickness narrowly escaped being murdered by an assassin sent by the Emir of Joppa. Having made a peace for nine years, he returned to Europe, and the ninth and last crusade was at an end.

71. The after fate of the Holy Land may be briefly told: The Christians, unmindful of their past sufferings and of the jealous neighbors they had to deal with, first broke the truce by plundering some Egyptian traders, near Margat. The Sultan revenged the outrage by taking possession of Margat, and war once more raged between the two nations. Tripoli and the other cities were captured in succession, until at last Acre was the only city of Palestine remaining to the Christians.

72. The Grand Master of the Templars collected his small and devoted band, and prepared to defend to the death the last possession of the order. Europe was deaf to his cry, the numbers of the foe were overwhelming, and devoted bravery was of no avail. In the disastrous siege the Christians were all but exterminated. The Grand Master fell at the head of his knights, pierced by many wounds. Seven Templars and as many Hospitallers alone escaped from the dreadful carnage. The victorious Moslems then set fire to the city, and the rule of the Christians in Palestine was brought to a close forever.

73. Kingsley ably summarizes the effects of the crusades as follow: "Egypt was still the center of communication between the two great stations of the Moslem power; and, indeed, as Mr. Lane has shown us in his most valuable translation of the 'Arabian Nights,' possessed a peculiar life and character of its own.

74. "It was the rash object of the crusaders to extinguish that life. Palestine was first their point of attack, but the later crusaders seem to have found, like all the

rest of the world, that the destinies of Palestine could not be separated from those of Egypt, and to Damietta accordingly was directed that last disastrous attempt of St. Louis. The crusaders failed utterly of the object at which they aimed. They succeeded in an object of which they never dreamed; for in those crusades the Moslem and the Christian had met face to face, and found that both were men, that they had a common humanity, a common eternal standard of nobility and virtue. So the Christian knights went home humbler and wiser men, when they found in the Saracen enemies the same generosity, truth, mercy, chivalrous self-sacrifice, which they fancied their own peculiar possession; and, added to that, a civilization and a learning which they could only admire and imitate. And, thus, from the era of the crusades, a kindlier feeling sprang up between the Crescent and the Cross, till it was again broken by the fearful invasions of the Turks through Eastern Europe.

75. "The learning of the Moslem, as well as their commerce, began to pour rapidly into Christendom, both from Spain, Egypt, and Syria; and thus the crusaders were, indeed, rewarded according to their deeds. They took the sword and perished by the sword. But the truly noble element in them, the element which our hearts and reasons recognize and love, in spite of all the folly and fanaticism of the crusades, whensoever we read 'Ivanhoe' or the 'Talisman,' the element of loyal faith and self-sacrifice, did not go unrequited.

76. "They learned wider, juster views of man and virtue, which I can not help believing must have had great effect in weakening in their minds the old, exclusive, bigoted notions, and in paving the way for the great outburst of free thought and the great assertion of the dignity of humanity which the fifteenth century beheld. They

opened a path for that influx of scientific knowledge which has produced in after centuries the most enormous effects on the welfare of Europe, and made life possible for millions who would otherwise have been pent within the narrow bounds of Europe to devour each other in the struggle for life and bread!"

CHAPTER III.

DEFENSE OF FREEDOM IN ALPINE PASSES.

1. While the great sovereigns of Europe were busy in fighting the Moslems in Palestine, they did not entirely neglect affairs at home. Some of them were very good rulers, protecting their subjects and maintaining good order, and others were tyrannical and imposed all sorts of taxes and heavy burdens upon the people. Up among the Alps, where the country is made up of rough, rocky mountains and narrow valleys, lived a people who were practically free. They lived in little communities, each one of which elected its own magistrate or governor, and made its own laws. The region was so poor and rough that the neighboring kings little cared to get possession of it, and the Alpine dwellers had a greater amount of freedom than any other people of Europe. The country was divided into little separate communities, one of which was called Schwytz, and this afterward gave the name to the whole country—Switzerland.

2. This country of the Swiss was really a part of the German empire, but the emperors had extended their rule over the lower parts of the country, leaving the forest cantons free. And a brave, courageous, and industrious people grew up there. No pauper-house among the Alps, for every able-bodied person worked, and no body tried to rob his neighbor of his honest earnings.

They were a strong athletic race, and the monarchs of the surrounding countries were glad to secure Swiss soldiers, for it was said that the Swiss never deserted. In 1298, while Wallace was struggling for freedom in Scotland, Albert of Austria, the second of the house of Hapsburg, resolved to get possession of the free forest cantons. He observed great secrecy in carrying out his designs, and it was not until a tax-gatherer or bailiff was permanently established in the country, supported by Austrian soldiers, that the people awakened to their danger. The story that follows is one that all true Swiss delight to believe, and, though it may not be true in regard to names and details, yet as a record of the main incidents of history it is substantially correct.

3. The first Austrian bailiff was Hermann Gessler, who built a strong fortress at Küssnacht, in Uri. At first he professed great love for the people, but when he became firmly established he threw off the mask, and showed himself to be a cruel, cowardly, mean-spirited tyrant. He was both vain and greedy, and he exacted both homage and tribute from the surrounding peasantry. Property was seized by the soldiers, and, should the owner venture to remonstrate, he was mercilessly beaten or killed on the spot. Complaints to the governor were followed by fresh outrages, until no one, even in the most secluded valleys, considered himself safe. Here tyranny as usual overstepped the bounds of safety. The free spirit, born of toil and privations in the mountain-fastnesses, would not long endure the outrages to which the people were subjected. A leader only was needed to induce a general revolt, and this leader was found in the person of William Tell.

4. William Tell, according to the received accounts, was born at Bürgelen, a secluded hamlet in the canton of

Lake Lucerne.

Uri, near the lake of Lucerne, about the year 1275; and, like his forefathers, was the proprietor of a cottage, a few small fields, a vineyard, and an orchard. When William had reached the age of twenty, his father is said to have died, bequeathing to him these humble possessions. Endowed by nature with a lofty and energetic mind, Tell was distinguished also by great physical strength and manly beauty. He was taller by a head than most of his companions; he loved to climb the rugged rocks of his native mountains in pursuit of the chamois, and to steer his boat across the lake in time of storm and of danger. The load of wood which he could bear upon his shoulders was double that which any ordinary man could support.

5. With other sources of happiness, Tell combined that of possessing an intimate friend, who dwelt amid the rocky heights separating Uri from Unterwalden. Arnold Anderhalden, of Melchthal, was this associate. Although similar in many salient points of character, there was still an essential difference between the two men. Arnold, of Melchthal, while he loved his country with an ardor equal to that of Tell, and was capable of very great actions, was not prepared for much patient suffering or long endurance of wrong. Tell, whose temperament was more calm, and whose passions were more influenced by reason than impulse, only succeeded in restraining his friend's impulsive character by the stern force of example. Meantime the two friends passed their days in the enjoyment of one another's society, visiting at intervals each other's humble residence. Tell foresaw, on the arrival of Gessler, many of the misfortunes which must inevitably follow his iron rule, and without explaining his views even to Arnold, of Melchthal, without needlessly alarming his family, endeavored to devise some means, not of bearing the yoke patiently, but of delivering his country from the galling

oppression which Albert had brought upon it. The hero felt satisfied that the evil deeds of the governor would sooner or later bring just retribution upon him; for this, and many other reasons, therefore, despite his own secret wishes, when Arnold poured out his fiery wrath in the ear of his friend, he listened calmly, and, to avoid inflaming him more, avowed none of his own views, or even feelings, in return.

6. One evening, however, William Tell and his wife sat in front of their cottage, watching their son amusing himself amid the flocks, when the former grew more thoughtful and sad than usual. Presently Tell spoke, and for the first time imparted to his wife some of his most secret designs. While the conversation was still proceeding, the parents saw their son rush toward them crying for help, and shouting the name of old Melchthal. As he spoke, Arnold's father appeared in sight, led by his grand-child, and feeling his way with a stick. Tell and his wife hastened forward, and discovered, to their inconceivable horror, that their friend was blind, his eyes having been put out with hot irons. The hero of Bürgelen, burning with just indignation, called on the old man to explain the fearful sight, and also the cause of Arnold's absence.

7. It appeared that that very morning the father, son, and grand-daughter were in the fields loading a couple of oxen with produce for the market-town, when an Austrian soldier presented himself, and, having examined the animals, which appeared to suit his fancy, ordered their owner to unyoke the beasts preparatory to his driving them off. Adding insolence to tyranny, he further remarked that such clod-poles might very well draw their own plows and carts. Arnold, furious at the man's daring impertinence, was only restrained by his father's ear-

nest entreaties from sacrificing the robber on the spot; nothing, however, could prevent him from aiming a blow at the soldier, which broke two of his fingers.

8. The enraged soldier then retreated; but old Melchthal, who well knew the character of Gessler, immediately forced Arnold, much against his inclination, to go and conceal himself for some days in the Righi. Scarcely had Arnold departed in this direction, when a detachment of guards from Altorf surrounded their humble tenement, and dragged old Melchthal before Gessler, who ordered him to give up his son. Furious at the refusal which ensued, the tyrant commanded the old man's eyes to be put out, and then sent him forth blind to deplore his misfortunes.

9. Tell heard the story of Melchthal in silence, and, when he had finished, inquired the exact spot of his son's concealment. The father replied that it was in a particular cavern of Mount Righi, the desert rocks of which place are unknown to the emissaries of the governor, and there he had promised to remain until he received his parent's permission to come forth. This Tell requested might be granted immediately; and, turning to his son, ordered him to start at once for the Righi with a message to Arnold. Walter obeyed gladly; and, providing himself with food, and receiving private instructions from his father, went on his journey under cover of the night.

10. Tell himself then threw around his own person a cloak of wolf-skin, seized his quiver full of sharp arrows, and, taking his terrible bow, which few could bend, in hand, bade adieu to his wife for a few days, and took his departure in an opposite direction from that pursued by his son. It was quite dawn when Walter reached the Righi, and a slight column of blue smoke speedily directed him to the spot where Arnold lay concealed. The intru-

sion at first startled the fugitive; but, recognizing Tell's son, he listened eagerly to his dismal story, the conclusion of which roused in him so much fury that he would have rushed forth at once to assassinate Gessler had not Walter restrained him.

11. Schooled by Tell, he informed him that his father was engaged in preparing vengeance for the tyrant's crime, being at that moment with Werner Stauffacher concerting proper measures of resistance. "'Go,' said my father, 'and tell Arnold of this new villany of the governor's, and say that it is not rage which can give us just revenge, but the utmost exertion of courage and prudence. I leave Schwytz to bid Werner arm his canton; let Melchthal go to Stautz and prepare the men of Unterwalden for the outbreak; having done this, let him meet me, with Fürst and Werner, in the field of Grütli!'"

12. Arnold, scarcely taking time to refresh himself with food, sent Walter on his homeward journey, while he started for Stautz. Walter, when alone, turned his steps toward Altorf, where unfortunately, and unknown to himself, he came into the presence of Gessler, to whom he uttered somewhat hard things about the state of the country, being led to commit himself by the artful questions of the tyrant, who immediately ordered the lad into confinement, with strict injunctions to the guards to seize whomsoever should claim him.

13. Meanwhile, certain doubts and fears, from he knew not what cause, arose in the mind of Gessler, and struck him with a presentiment that all was not right. He imagined that the people wore in their looks less abject submission to his authority, and, the better to satisfy himself of the correctness or erroneousness of this view, he commanded Berenger to erect at dawn of day, in the market-place of Altorf, a pole, on the point of which he was to

place the ducal cap of Austria. An order was further promulgated, to the effect that every one passing near or within sight of it should make obeisance, in proof of his honor and fealty to the duke.

14. Numerous soldiers under arms were directed to surround the place, to keep the avenues, and to compel the passers-by to bend with proper respect to the emblem of the governing power of the three cantons. Gessler likewise determined that whoever should disobey the mandate should be accused of disaffection, and treated accordingly; a measure which promised both to discover the discontented, and furnish sufficient grounds for their punishment. Numerous detachments of troops, among whom money had been previously distributed, were then placed around to see that his commands were scrupulously obeyed. History scarcely records another instance of tyranny so galling and humiliating to the oppressed, and so insolent on the part of its author.

15. The proceedings of Tell in the interval were of the deepest concern to the country. Having arrived within the territory of Schwytz, and at the village of Stainea, he called at the house of Werner, and, being admitted, threw at his feet a heavy bundle of lances, arrows, cross-bows, and swords. "Werner Stauffacher," cried Tell, "the time is come for action!" and without a moment's delay he informed his friend of all that had passed, dwelling minutely on every detail. And, when he had at length finished, the cautious Werner could restrain his wrath no longer, but exclaimed, clasping the hero's hand, "Friend, let us begin; I am ready!" After further brief conference, they, by separate ways, carried round arms to their friends in the town and neighboring villages. Many hours were thus consumed; and, when their weapons were at last distributed, they both returned to Stauffacher's house,

snatched some slight refreshment, and then sped on their way to Grütli, accompanied by ten of their most tried adherents.

16. The lake of Lucerne was soon reached, and a boat procured. Werner, perceiving the furious tempest, inquired of Tell if his skill would enable him to struggle against the storm. "Arnold awaits us!" cried William; "and the fate of our country depends on this interview!" With these words he leaped into the boat, Werner jumped after him, and the rest followed. Tell cast loose the agitated vessel, seized the tiller, and, hoisting sail, the little craft flew along the waves.

17. Presently, it is said, the wind moderated, and ere they reached the opposite side had ceased altogether—a phenomenon common in these mountain lakes. The boat was now made fast, and the conspirators hastened to the field of Grütli, where, at the mouth of a cavern of the same name, Arnold and Walter Fürst awaited them, each with ten other companions. Tell allowed no consideration of natural feeling to silence the calls of duty, but at once came to the point. He first gave a brief sketch of the state of the country under the Austrian bailiffs, and, having shown to the satisfaction of his companions the necessity for immediate and combined action, is related to have added: "We may have our plans frustrated by delay, and the time has come for action. I ask only a few days for preparation. Unterwalden and Schwytz are armed. Three hundred and fifty warriors are, I am assured, ready. I will remain in Altorf, and, as soon as I receive tidings from Früst, will fire a huge pile of wood near my house. At this signal let all march to the rendezvous, and, when united, we will pour down upon Altorf, where I will then strive to rouse the people!"

18. This plan of the campaign was agreed to; and it

was further resolved that, in the enterprise upon which they were now embarked, no one should be guided by his own private opinion, nor ever forsake his friends; that they should jointly live or jointly die in defense of the common cause; that each should in his own vicinity promote the object in view, trusting that the whole nation would one day have cause to bless their friendly union; that the Count of Hapsburg should be deprived of none of his lands, vassals, or prerogatives; that the freedom which they had inherited from their fathers they were determined to assert, and to hand down to their children untainted and undiminished. Then Stauffacher, Fürst, and Melchthal, and the other conspirators, stepped forward, and, raising their hands, swore that they would die in defense of that freedom. After this solemn oath, and after an agreement that New Year's Day should be chosen for the outbreak, unless, in the meantime, a signal fire should arouse the inhabitants on some sudden emergency, the heroes separated. Arnold returned to Stautz, Werner to Schwytz, while Tell and Fürst took their way to Altorf. The sun already shone brightly as Tell entered the town, and he at once advanced into the public place, where the first object which caught his eye was a handsome cap embroidered with gold stuck upon the end of a long pole. Soldiers walked around it in respectful silence, and the people of Altorf, as they passed, bowed their heads profoundly to the symbol of power.

19. Tell was much surprised at this new and strange manifestation of servility, and, leaning on his cross-bow, gazed contemptuously both on the people and the soldiers. Berenger, captain of the guard, at length observed this man, who alone, amid a cringing populace, carried his head erect. He went to him, and fiercely asked why he neglected to pay obedience to the orders of Hermann

Gessler? Tell replied that he saw no reason why he should bow to a hat, or even to the one which the hat represented. This bold language surprised Berenger, who ordered Tell to be disarmed, and then, surrounded by guards, he was carried before the governor. "Wherefore," demanded the incensed bailiff, "hast thou disobeyed my orders, and failed in thy respect to the emperor? Why hast thou dared to pass before the sacred badge of thy sovereign without the evidence of homage required of thee?" "Verily," answered Tell, with mock humility, "how this happened I know not; "'tis an accident, and no mark of contempt. Suffer me, therefore, in thy clemency to depart."

20. Gessler was irritated at this reply, feeling assured that there was something beneath the tranquil and bitter smile of the prisoner which he could not fathom. Suddenly he was struck by the resemblance which existed between him and the boy Walter, whom he had met the previous day, and immediately ordered him to be brought forward.

21. Gessler now inquired the prisoner's name, which he no sooner learned than he recognized as that of the archer so celebrated throughout the canton. As soon as the youth arrived, the governor turned to Tell and told him that he had heard of his extraordinary dexterity, and was accordingly determined to put it to proof. "While beholding justice done, the people of Altorf shall also admire thy skill. Thy son shall be placed a hundred yards distant, with an apple on his head; if thou hast the good fortune to carry off the apple in triumph with one of thy arrows, I pardon both, and restore your liberty. If thou refusest this trial, thy son shall die before thine eyes!"

22. Tell implored Gessler to spare him so cruel an experiment, but, finding the governor inexorable, the hero

submitted to the trial. He was conducted into the public place, where the required distance was measured by Berenger—a double row of soldiers shutting up three sides of the square. The people, awe-stricken and trembling, pressed behind. Walter stood with his back to a linden-tree, patiently awaiting the exciting moment. Hermann Gessler, some distance behind, watched every motion. His cross-bow and belt were handed to Tell; he tried the point, broke the weapon, and demanded his quiver. It was brought to him, and emptied at his feet. William stooped down, and, taking a long time to choose one, managed to hide a second in his girdle; the other he held in his hand, and proceeded to string his bow, while Berenger cleared away the remaining arrows. After hesitating, he drew the bow, aimed, shot, and the apple, struck through the core, was carried away by the arrow.

23. The market-place was filled by loud cries of admiration. Walter flew to embrace his father, who, overcome by the excess of his emotions, fell insensible to the ground, thus exposing the second arrow to view. Gessler stood over him awaiting his recovery, which speedily took place. Tell rose, and turned away from the governor, who, however, thus addressed him: "Incomparable archer! I will keep my promise; but," added he, "tell me what needed you with that second arrow which you have, I see, secreted in your girdle? One was surely enough." "The second shaft," replied Tell, "was to pierce thy heart, tyrant, if I had chanced to harm my son!" At these words the terrified governor retired behind his guards, revoked his promise of pardon, commanding him further to be placed in irons, and to be reconducted to the fort. He was obeyed, and, as slight murmurs rose among the people, double patrols of Austrian soldiers paraded the streets, and forced the citizens to retire to their houses. Walter,

released, fled to join Arnold, of Melchthal, according to a whispered order from his father.

24. Gessler, reflecting on the aspect of the people, and fearful that some plot was in progress, which his accidental shortness of provisions rendered more unfortunate, determined to rid his citadel of the object which might induce an attack. With this in view, he summoned Berenger, and said to him: "I am about to leave Altorf, and you shall command during my absence. I leave my brave soldiers, who will readily obey your voice; and soon, returning with supplies and reinforcements, we will crush this vile people, and punish them for their insolent murmurings. Prepare me a large boat, in which thirty men, picked from my guard, may depart with me. As soon as night comes on, load this audacious Tell with chains, and send him on board. I will myself take him where he can expiate his crimes!"

25. The evening was fine and promising; the boat danced along the placid waters. The air was pure, the waves tranquil, the stars shone brightly in the sky. A light southern breeze aided the efforts of the oarsmen, and tempered the rigor of the cold, which night in that season rendered almost insupportable so near the glaciers. All appeared in Gessler's favor. The extent of the first section of the lake was soon passed, and the boat headed for Brunnen. Tell, meantime, loaded with irons, gazed with eager eye on the desert rocks of Grütli, where the day before he had planned with his friends for the deliverance of his country. While painful thoughts crossed his mind, his looks were attracted by a dim light which burst forth near his own house. Presently this light increased, and before long a blaze arose visible all over Uri. The heart of the prisoner beat with joy, for he felt that all efforts were making to rescue him. Gessler observed

the flame, which in reality was a signal-fire to arouse the cantons, but supposed it some Swiss peasant's house accidentally in flames.

26. Suddenly, however, between Fluelen and Sissigen, when in deep water, intermingled with shoals, the south wind ceased to blow, and one of those storms which are common on the lake commenced. A north wind burst upon them, raised the waves to a great height, and dashed them over the gunwale of the boat, which, giving way to the fury of the storm, flew toward the shore that, rocky and precipitous, menaced their lives. The bleak wind brought also frost, snow, and sleet, which spread darkness over the waters, and covered the hands and faces of the rowers with ice. The soldiers, inert and panic-stricken, prayed for life, while Gessler, but ill prepared for death, was profuse in his offers of money and other rewards if they would rouse themselves to save him.

27. In this emergency the Austrian bailiff was reminded by one of his attendants that the prisoner Tell was no less skillful in the management of a boat than in the exercise of the bow. "And, see, my lord," said one of the men, representing to Gessler the imminent peril they were all incurring, "all are paralyzed with terror, and even the pilot is unable to manage the helm!"

28. Gessler's fear of Tell induced him at first to hesitate, but, the prayers of the soldiers becoming pressing, he told the prisoner that if he could take them safely through the storm he should be at once unbound. Tell having replied that, by the grace of God, he could still save them, was instantly freed from his shackles and placed at the helm, when the boat, answering to a master-hand, kept its course steadily through the bellowing surge, as if conscious of the free spirit which had now taken the command.

29. Guiding the obedient tiller at his will, Tell pointed the head of the boat in the direction whence they came, which he knew to be the only safe course; and, encouraging and cheering the rowers, made rapid and steady progress through the water. The darkness which now wrapped them round prevented Gessler from discovering that he had turned his back on his destination. Tell continued on his way nearly the whole night, the dying light of the signal-fire on the mountain serving as a beacon in enabling him to approach the shores of Schwytz, and to avoid the shoals.

30. Between Sissigen and Fluelen are two mountains, the greater and the lesser Achsenberg, whose sides, hemmed in and rising perpendicularly from the bed of the lake, offer not a single platform where human foot can stand. When near this place dawn broke in the eastern sky, and Gessler—the danger appearing to decrease—scowled upon Tell in sullen silence. As the prow of the vessel was driven inland, Tell perceived a solitary table-rock, and called to the rowers to redouble their efforts till they should have passed the precipice ahead, observing with ominous truth that it was the most dangerous pòint on the whole lake.

31. The soldiers here recognized their position, and pointed it out to Gessler, who demanded of Tell what he meant by taking them back to Altorf. William, without answering him, brought the bow suddenly close upon the rock, seized his bow, and, with an effort which sent the unguided craft back into the lake, sprang on shore, scaled the rocks, and took the direction of Schwytz.

32. Having thus escaped the clutches of the governor, he made for the main road between Art and Küssnacht, and there hid himself until such a time as the bailiff should pass that way. Gessler and his attendants having, with

great difficulty, effected a landing at Brunnen, proceeded toward Küssnacht. In the spot still known as "the hollow way," and marked by a chapel, Tell overheard the threats pronounced against himself should he once more be caught, and, in default of his apprehension, vengeance was vowed against his family. Tell felt that the safety of himself and his wife and children, to say nothing of the duty he owed to his country, required the tyrant's death; and, seizing an arrow, he pierced Gessler to the heart.

33. The bold deed accomplished, the hero effected his escape to Stemen, where he found Werner Stauffacher preparing to march. Immediate action was now necessary, but the original decision of the conspirators remained unchanged. Accordingly, on the morning of New Year's Day, 1308, the castle of Rostberg, in Obwalden, was taken possession of, its keeper, Berenger, of Landasberg, made prisoner, and compelled to promise that he would never again set foot within the territory of the three cantons, after which he was allowed to retire to Lucerne.

34. Stauffacher, the same morning, at the head of the men of Schwytz, destroyed the fortress of Schwanan, while Tell and the men of Uri took possession of Altorf. On the following Sunday the deputies of Uri, Schwytz, and Unterwalden met, and renewed that fraternal league which has endured to this day.

35. In 1315 Leopold, second son of Albert, determined to punish the confederate cantons for their revolt, and accordingly marched against them at the head of a considerable army, accompanied by a numerous retinue of nobles. Count Otho, of Strasberg, one of his ablest generals, crossed the Brunig with a body of four thousand men, intending to attack Upper Unterwalden. The bailiffs of Willisan, of Wodhausen, and of Lucerne meantime

armed a fourth of that number to make a descent on the lower division of the same canton, while the emperor in person, at the head of his army of reserve, poured down from Egerson on Mogarten, in the country of Schwytz, ostentatiously displaying an extensive supply of rope wherewith to hang the chiefs of the rebels.

36. The confederates, in order to oppose this formidable invasion, occupied a position in the mountains bordering on the convent of Our Lady of the Hermits. Four hundred men of Uri, and three hundred of Unterwalden, had effected a junction with the warriors of Schwytz, who formed the principal force of the little army. Fifty men, banished from this latter canton, offered themselves to combat beneath their banner, intending to efface by their valor the remembrance of past faults. Early on the morning of November 15, 1315, some thousands of well-armed Austrian knights slowly ascended the hill on which the Swiss were posted, with the hope of dislodging them; the latter, however, advanced to meet their enemies, uttering the most terrific cries. The band of banished men, having precipitated large stones and fragments of rocks from the hillsides and from overhanging cliffs, rushed from behind the sheltering influence of a thick fog and threw the advancing columns into confusion. The Austrians immediately broke their ranks, and presently a complete rout, with terrible slaughter, ensued. The flower of the Austrian chivalry perished on the field of Morgarten, beneath the halberts, arrows, and iron-headed clubs of the shepherds. Leopold, himself, though he succeeded in gaining the shattered remnant of his forces, had a narrow escape, while the Swiss, animated by victory, hastened to Unterwalden, where they defeated another body of Austrians. In this instance Count Otho had as narrow an escape as the emperor.

37. After these two well-fought fields, the confederates hastened to renew their ancient alliance, which was solemnly sworn to in an assembly held at Brunnen on the eighth day of December.

38. After the battle of Morgarten one canton after another threw off the Austrian yoke, and joined the forest cantons, until nearly all Switzerland was joined in a confederacy. A later war waged by Albert proved disastrous to the Austrian cause, and ended by a further consolidation of the Swiss cantons. In 1386, seventy years after Morgarten, the Austrians made another attempt to bring the brave mountaineers into subjection. An army of nine thousand men, the best trained soldiers of the empire, under the lead of the Archduke Leopold, invaded the country. To these the confederates opposed a force of fourteen hundred. They met in a valley near the lake of Sempach. The Austrians had learned something of Swiss warfare, and knew that they stood no chance in a hand-to-hand conflict with the Swiss, and so they formed their men into squares, with a wall of bristling spears on every side. Upon this solid mass of men the Swiss could make no impression. In vain they charged with the fiery courage which had so often gained them the victory; they could find no vulnerable point in the serried columns, and it seemed that the brave mountaineers must all perish, and leave their homes again to the mercy of the Austrian soldiers. But, when almost in despair, the tide of battle was turned by the acts of a single Swiss soldier, Arnold Winkelried, of Unterwalden. He communicated his plan to his immediate neighbors, and then, rushing forward, he grasped as many of the Austrian spears as he could reach; and, gathering them together, he bowed to the ground with the spears buried in his breast. Into the breach his companions rushed, and with their powerful

swords they soon widened the space, so that the whole Swiss force had room for action. The Austrians were almost annihilated, Leopold himself being slain. The poet Montgomery has given the following version of this event:

ARNOLD WINKELRIED.

39. "Make way for liberty!" he cried;
"Make way for liberty!" and died.

40. In arms the Austrian phalanx stood,
A living wall, a human wood!
A wall where every conscious stone
Seemed to its kindred thousands grown;
A rampart all assaults to bear,
Till time to dust their frames should wear!
A wood, like that enchanted grove
In which with fiends Rinaldo strove,
Where every silent tree possessed
A spirit prisoned in its breast,
Which the first stroke of coming strife
Would startle into hideous life;
So dense, so still, the Austrians stood,
A living wall, a human wood!
Impregnable their front appears,
All horrent with projected spears,
Whose polished points before them shine,
From flank to flank, one brilliant line,
Bright as the breakers' splendors run
Along the billows, to the sun.

41. Opposed to these, a hovering band
Contended for their native land;
Peasants, whose new-found strength had broke
From manly necks the ignoble yoke,

And forged their fetters into swords,
On equal terms to fight their lords:
And what insurgent rage had gained,
In many a mortal fray maintained!
Marshaled at morn at Freedom's call,
They come to conquer or to fall,
Where he who conquered, he who fell,
Was deemed a dead, or living Tell!
Such virtue had that patriot breathed,
So to the soil his soul bequeathed,
That wheresoe'er his arrows flew,
Heroes in his own likeness grew,
And warriors sprang from every sod
Which his awakening footstep trod.

42. And now the work of life and death
Hung on the passing of a breath;
The fire of conflict burnt within,
The battle trembled to begin;
Yet, while the Austrians held their ground,
Point for attack was nowhere found.
Where'er the impatient Switzers gazed,
The unbroken line of lances blazed;
That line 'twere suicide to meet,
And perish at their tyrant's feet:
How could they rest within their graves,
And leave their homes the homes of slaves?
Would they not feel their children tread
With clanging chains above their head?

43. It must not! This day, this hour,
Annihilates the oppressor's power;
All Switzerland is in the field,

She will not fly, she can not yield—
She must not fall; her better fate
Here gives her an immortal date.
Few were the numbers she could boast;
But every freeman was a host,
And felt as though himself were he
On whose sole arm hung victory!

44. It did depend on one, indeed,
Behold him—Arnold Winkelried!
There sounds not to the tramp of fame
The echo of a nobler name.
Unmarked he stood amid the throng,
In rumination deep and long,
Till you might see, with sudden grace,
The very thought come o'er his face,
And by the motion of his form
Anticipate the coming storm;
And by the uplifting of his brow
Tell where the bolt would strike, and how.

45. But 'twas no sooner thought and done,
The field was in a moment won.

46. "Make way for Liberty!" he cried;
Then ran with arms extended wide
As if his dearest friend to clasp;
Ten spears he swept within his grasp.
"Make way for Liberty!" he cried:
Their keen points met from side to side;
He bowed among them like a tree,
And thus made way for Liberty!

47. Swift to the breach his comrades fly;
"Make way for Liberty!" they cry.

And through the Austrian phalanx dart,
As rushed the spears through Arnold's heart!
While instantaneous as his fall,
Rout, ruin, panic, scattered all:
An earthquake could not overthrow
A city with a surer blow.

48. Thus Switzerland again was free,
Thus death made way for Liberty!

49. In the next fifty years the Swiss were engaged in a war with Austria and another with France, and in both cases they were victorious. But, while they were exhausted by the incessant wars that had been urged upon them, they were threatened with a more formidable invasion than ever. Charles the Bold, Duke of Burgundy, resolved to attach Switzerland to his domain. Crossing the Jura, the duke found himself in possession of Yverdun, it having been betrayed into his hands; but the citadel still held out. Charles, irritated that his progress should be stayed by such a handful of men, offered to let them retire home if they would surrender, but if they still held out he would hang them all! The Swiss, knowing prolonged defense was useless, surrendered. As they marched out of the citadel they were seized, by order of the duke, and all murdered.

50. Aroused by these horrors, an army of twenty thousand advanced to meet the duke at the head of three times that number. In the battle that ensued the Burgundians were entirely defeated, and Charles narrowly escaped with his life. Writhing under his disgrace, and vowing revenge, the duke raised a much more numerous army, and again invaded Switzerland.

51. He advanced by the way of the lake of Neufchatel,

and paused a few days to capture the fortress on the banks of Lake Morat. While the siege was going on the Swiss army concentrated, and marched to meet their foes. Thirty thousand men were to fight the battle of freedom against one hundred thousand. It was on Saturday, June 22, 1476. The weather was threatening, the sky overcast, and rain fell in torrents. A vanguard was formed, commanded by John Hallwyl, who knelt and besought a blessing from on high. While they yet prayed the sun broke through the clouds, upon which the Swiss commander rose, sword in hand, crying: "Up, up, Heaven smiles on our victory!" The artillery thundered forth as he spoke, and the whole plain, from the lake to the rocky heights, became one vast battle-field! Toward the main body of the Burgundians the Swiss army poured down with irresistible force and courage; and, clearing all difficulties, they reached the line of the enemy. A fearful slaughter now ensued. The Burgundians were utterly vanquished. The haughty duke, pale and dispirited, fled with a few followers, and never stopped till he reached the banks of Lake Leman. The rout was so complete that many of the Burgundians, in terror and despair, threw themselves into the Lake of Morat, the banks of which were strewed with the bodies of the slain.

52. The battle of Morat lives in history with the victories of Marathon and Bannockburn. In each, freedom for the nation was secured, and liberty for man was preserved and transmitted. As a deed, the Swiss victory for ever freed a people from a grasping foreign tyrant; and it is a matter of rejoicing to all who love liberty till to-day, and, like other great events, it is the subject of national traditions.

53. According to one of these, a young native of Friburg, who had been engaged in the battle, keenly desirous

of being the first to carry home tidings of the victory, ran the whole way—a distance of ten or twelve miles—and with such overhaste that on his arrival at the market-place he dropped with fatigue, and, barely able to shout that the Swiss were victorious, immediately expired. A twig of lime-tree, which he carried in his hand, was planted on the spot in commemoration of this event; and till the present day are seen, in the market-place of Friburg, the aged and propped-up remains of the venerable tree which grew from this twig. In most of the towns of Switzerland a "tree of Liberty" is preserved, which came from scions of the original tree at Friburg.

CHAPTER IV.

BRUCE AND BANNOCKBURN.

1. Six hundred years ago the duty of defending freedom fell to King Robert Bruce and the Scotch. And this is how it happened. The time was during the crusades, when all Europe was marching to the East, and engaging in battle with the Moslems. Scotland had been an independent country for many years, but some of her princes were too weak for those troublous times. The witches that deceived Macbeth seem to have cast a spell upon the prosperity of the country. Clan was at enmity with clan, and one great chieftain waged relentless war with another. The fierce nobles paid little heed to the king, and showed no regard for the rights of the people. It seemed that peace and liberty had departed forever.

2. Alexander III died, leaving no direct heir. The Scottish nobles assembled to elect who should be their king. The choice lay between Robert Bruce and John Balliol. As the nobles could not agree, the matter was referred to King Edward I, of England, who decided in favor of Balliol. The new prince was weak, and, when he resented the interference of King Edward in some of his affairs, he was easily defeated and driven from the kingdom. Scotland was now regarded as a conquered country, and the people were terribly oppressed. The nobles were deprived of their estates, and the poor peo-

ple were taxed to the verge of starvation. For fifteen years King Edward held on to his usurped power, while the weak king Balliol was wandering in foreign lands, paying no attention to the distracted state of his country.

3. At last the oppression became so great that conflicts took place almost daily between the Scotch peasants and the English soldiery. On one occasion, a young man named William Wallace was out a-fishing with a boy to carry the fish. Two or three English soldiers came along and insisted on taking the fish. Wallace offered to divide with them, but they insisted on taking the whole, when he flew in a rage, killed one with his fishing-pole, and, seizing a sword, put the others to flight. He then fled, and concealed himself in the mountains until the matter blew over. On another occasion he killed an Englishman who insulted him at a fair, and fled to his home, where he was pursued by the soldiers. He escaped by the back door, but the cruel English leader, Hazelrigg, put his wife and servants to death. From that time Wallace devoted himself to fighting the English. He soon collected a band of outlaws and attacked the English whereever he found a favorable opportunity. He soon had the satisfaction of killing Hazelrigg, and of capturing many important places.

4. The Scotch rose everywhere and joined Wallace, who soon found himself at the head of a formidable army. With this he captured the English fortresses, and finally defeated the chief English army under Earl Warren. Scotland was now free, but the English king hastened back from Flanders to punish the Scotch. The battle of Falkirk was fought July 22, 1298, and the Scotch were entirely defeated. Wallace again became a fugitive, but was betrayed into the hands of Edward,

and was beheaded and quartered, according to the barbarous custom of the times.

5. The eyes of all Scotland were now turned to Robert Bruce as the only remaining champion who would be likely to make head against the English, and he accepted the proffered leadership. His principal rival was a powerful noble called the Red Comyn, and with this rival Bruce sought to make friends. The two met in a church, and Comyn flatly refused to join the Scottish cause, but openly proclaimed his adherence to the English. A quarrel arose, and, in the excitement, Bruce stabbed Comyn. Almost paralyzed at his act, he rushed out of the house and called for his horse. His friends eagerly inquired what was the matter. "I doubt," said Bruce, "that I have slain the Red Comyn." "Do not leave the matter in doubt," said Kirkpatrick; "I will make it certain." He and his companions then rushed into the church and soon dispatched Comyn with their daggers.

6. This deed is the one great blot upon the name of Bruce, and bitterly did he repent of his rashness. It called down upon his devoted head the anathema of the church for sacrilege in committing violence before the holy altar. It arrayed against him the kinsmen and friends of the Red Comyn, and it produced distrust in the minds of many true friends of Scotland, who could never have confidence in such an impetuous leader. Bruce made a vow that, if he succeeded in securing the freedom of Scotland, he would do penance for his crime by entering upon a crusade and fighting for the holy sepulchre.

7. On the 29th of March, 1306, Bruce was crowned king. His enemies immediately attacked and defeated him, and he was obliged to take refuge in the mountains of the Highlands. Here he was hunted like a wild

animal, and was obliged to flee from one fastness to another. One of the most malignant of his enemies was Lord Lorn, a kinsman of the Red Comyn. At one time Bruce and his few followers were retreating through a narrow pass, when he was set upon by Lorn and a much superior force. Sending his followers ahead, he stopped his horse in the narrow way, and covered their retreat. Upon seeing the king thus alone, three powerful highlandmen—a father and two sons—set upon him, determined to kill him or take him prisoner for their master, Lord Lorn. Bruce struck the first man who came up and seized his bridle such a blow with his sword as to cut off his hand and free the bridle. The man bled to death. The other brother seized him by the leg and attempted to throw him from his horse. The king, setting spurs to the horse, made the animal spring forward so that the Highlander fell under the horse's feet, and, as he endeavored to rise, the king cleft his head in two with his sword. The father, seeing his two sons thus slain, flew at Bruce and grasped him in his mantle so close to his body that he could not have room to wield his long sword. But, with an iron hammer which hung at his saddle-bow, Bruce dashed out the brains of this new assailant. The dying man still clung to the king's mantle, so that, to get free, Bruce was obliged to undo the brooch by which it was fastened, and leave it with the mantle behind. This brooch fell into the hands of Lorn, and was kept in the family for many generations as a memorial of Bruce.

8. But Bruce was soon reduced to greater straits, and, without followers, was obliged to conceal himself in stables and caves. In all his misfortunes he never gave up the cause of his country, and he sacredly devoted his life to the freedom of Scotland. After one of his defeats he

was lying one night on a wretched bed in a rude hut, while debating in his own mind whether it were not best to enlist in a crusade, when his attention was directed to a spider on the rafters overhead. He saw that the little spinner was trying to swing from one rafter to another, so as to fix his thread across the space. Time and again it tried and failed. Admiring the perseverance of the creature, Bruce began to count the number of times he tried. One, two, three, four, five, six. It suddenly occurred to Bruce that this was just the number of times he had failed in his attempts against the enemy. He then made up his mind that if the spider succeeded in the next trial he would make one more endeavor to recover his kingdom, but if it failed he would start at once for Palestine. The spider sprang into the air, and this time succeeded, so the king resolved upon another trial, and never after met with a defeat.

9. Many a wild story is told of his feats of arms and hairbreadth escapes while he wandered about without a country. Sir Walter Scott, in his poem, "The Lord of the Isles," records one of these legends. It is reported that, on one occasion, with his brother Edward and sister Isabel in a boat, he was driven by stress of weather to take refuge in one of the Hebrides upon the western coast, the home of Roland, the Lord of the Isles. It happened to be a festive occasion, a large assembly having met to celebrate the marriage of the Lord of the Isles with the sister of the Lord of Lorn. As Bruce entered the banquet-hall, Lorn recognized him:

10. "Now, by Columba's shrine I swear,
And every saint that's buried there,
'Tis he himself!" Lorn sternly cries;
"And for my kinsman's death he dies!"

As loudly Roland calls, "Forbear!
Not in my sight while brand I wear,
O'ermatched by odds shall warrior fall,
Or blood of stranger stain my hall!
This ancient fortress of my race
Shall be misfortune's resting-place,
Shelter or shield of the distressed,
No slaughter-house of shipwrecked guest!"

11. "Talk not to me," fierce Lorn replied,
"Of odds or match! When Comyn died,
Three daggers clashed within his side!
Talk not to me of sheltering hall,
The church of God saw Comyn fall!
On God's own altar streamed his blood,
While o'er my prostrate kinsman stood
The ruthless murderer—e'en as now—
With armèd hand and scornful brow!
Up, all who love me! blow on blow,
And lay the outlawed felons low!"

. . . . . .

12. Then waked the wild debate again,
With brawling threat and clamor vain,
Vassals and menials thronging in,
Lent their brute rage to swell the din;
When far and wide a bugle clang
From the dark ocean upward rang.
"The abbot comes!" they cried at once,
"The holy man whose favored glance
  Hath sainted visions known;
Angels have met him on the way,
Beside the blessed martyr's bay,
  And by Columba's stone.

He comes our feuds to reconcile,
A sainted man from sainted isle;
We will his holy will abide,
The abbot shall our strife decide!"

13. The abbot on the threshold stood,
And in his hands the holy rood;
Back on his shoulders flowed his hood,
  The torch's glaring ray
Showed, in its red and flashing light,
His withered cheek and amice white,
His blue eye glistening cold and bright,
  His tresses scant and gray.
"Fair lords," he said, "our lady's love,
And peace be with you from above,
  And benedicite!
But what means this? no peace is here!
Do dirks unsheathed suit bridal cheer?
  Or are these naked brands
A seemly show for churchman's sight,
When he comes summoned to unite
  Betrothèd hearts and hands?"
Then, cloaking hate with fiery zeal,
Proud Lorn answered the appeal:
  "Thou comest, O holy man,
True sons of blessed church to greet,
But little deeming here to meet
  A wretch, beneath the ban
Of pope and church, for murder done
Even on the sacred altar-stone!
Well may'st thou wonder we should know
Such miscreant here, nor lay him low,
Or dream of greeting, peace, or truce,
With excommunicated Bruce!

Yet will I grant, to end debate,
Thy sainted voice decide his fate."

14. Then Roland pled the stranger's cause
And knighthood's oath and honor's laws;
And Isabel on bended knee
Brought prayers and tears to back her plea;
And Edith lent her generous aid,
And wept, and Lorn for mercy prayed.

15. Then Argentine, in England's name,
So highly urged his sovereign's claim,
He waked a spark, that, long suppressed,
Had smoldered in Lord Roland's breast;
And now, as from the flint the fire,
Flashed forth at once his generous ire:
"Enough of noble blood," he said,
"By English Edward had been shed,
Since matchless Wallace first had been
In mockery crowned with wreaths of green,
And done to death by felon hand,
For guarding well his native land.
Where's Nigel Bruce? and De la Haye,
And valiant Seaton—where are they?
Where Somerville, the kind and free?
And Fraser, flower of chivalry?
Have they not been on gibbet bound,
Their quarters flung to hawk and hound,
And hold we here a cold debate
To yield more victims to their fate?
What! can the English leopard's mood
Never be gorged with Northern blood?
Was not the life of Athole shed
To soothe the tyrant's sickened bed?

Nor must his word, till dying day,
Be nought but quarter, hang, and slay?"

16. "Nor deem," said Dunnegan's knight,
"That thou shalt brave alone the fight!
By saints of isle and mainland both,
By woden wild—my grandsire's oath—
Let Rome and England do their worst;
Howe'er attainted and accursed,
If Bruce shall e'er find friends again,
Once more to brave a battle-plain,
If Douglas couch again his lance,
Or Randolph dare another chance,
Old Torquil will not be to lack
With twice a thousand at his back;
Nay, chafe not at my bearing bold,
Good abbot! for thou knowest of old,
Torquil's rude thought and stubborn will
Smack of the wild Norwegian still:
Nor will I barter freedom's cause
For England's wealth or Rome's applause!"

17. The abbot seemed with eye severe,
The hardy chieftain's speech to hear;
Then on King Robert turned the monk,
But twice his courage came and sunk,
Confronted with the hero's look;
Twice fell his eye, his accents shook;
At length resolved in tone and brow,
Sternly he questioned him, "And thou
Unhappy, what hast thou to plead,
Why I denounce not on thy deed
That awful doom which canons tell
Shuts paradise and opens hell?

Anathema of power so dread,
It blends the living with the dead,
Bids each good angel soar away,
And every ill one claim his prey;
Expels thee from the church's care,
And deafens Heaven against thy prayer;
Arms every hand against thy life,
Bans all who aid thee in the strife;
Nay, each whose succor, cold and scant,
With meanest alms relieves thy want;
Haunts thee when living; and, when dead,
Dwells on thy yet devoted head,
Rends honor's 'scutcheon from thy hearse,
Stills o'er thy bier the holy verse,
And spurns thy corpse from hallowed ground,
Flung like vile carrion to the hound;
Such is the dire and desperate doom
For sacrilege, decreed by Rome;
And such the well-deserved meed
Of thine unhallowed, ruthless deed."

18. "Abbot!" the Bruce replied, "thy charge
It boots me not to dispute at large;
This much, howe'er, I bid thee know,
No selfish vengeance dealt the blow,
For Comyn died his country's foe.
Nor blame I friends whose ill-timed speed
Fulfilled my soon-repented deed,
Nor censure those from whose stern tongue,
The dire anathema has rung.
I only blame my own wild ire,
By Scotland's wrongs incensed to fire.
Heaven knows my purpose to atone,
Far as I may, the evil done,

Edinburgh Castle.

And hears a penitent's appeal,
From papal curse and prelate zeal.
My first and dearest task achieved,
Fair Scotland from her thrall relieved,
Shall many a priest in cope and stole
Say requiem for Red Comyn's soul,
While I the blessèd cross advance,
And expiate this unhappy chance
In Palestine, with sword and lance.
But, while content the church should know
My conscience owns the debt I owe,
Unto de Argentine and Lorn
The name of traitor I return,
Bid them defiance, stern and high,
And give them in their throats the lie!
These brief words spoke, I speak no more,
Do as thou wilt; my shrift is o'er."

19. Like man by prodigy amazed,
Upon the king the abbot gazed;
Then o'er his pallid features glance
Convulsions of ecstatic trance.
His breathing came more thick and fast,
And from his pale-blue eyes were cast
Strange rays of wild and wandering light;
Uprise his locks of silver white,
Flushed is his brow, through every vein
In azure tides the currents strain,
And undistinguished accents broke
The awful silence e'er he spoke.

20. "De Bruce, I rose with purpose dread
To speak my curse upon thy head,

And give thee as an outcast o'er
To him who burns to shed thy gore;
But like the Midianite of old
Who stood on Zophin, heaven-controlled,
I feel within my aged breast
A power that can not be repressed.
It prompts my voice, it swells my veins,
It burns, it maddens, it constrains!
De Bruce, thy sacrilegious blow
Hath at God's altar slain thy foe;
O'ermastered, yet by high behest,
I bless thee, and thou shalt be blest!"
He spoke, and o'er the astonished throng
Was silence, awful, deep and long.
Again that light has fired his eye,
Again his form swells bold and high,
The broken voice of age is gone,
'Tis vigorous manhood's lofty tone:
"Thrice vanquished on the battle-plain,
Thy followers slaughtered, fled, or ta'en,
A hunted wanderer on the wild,
On foreign shores a man exiled,
Disowned, deserted, and distressed,
I bless thee, and thou shalt be blessed!
Blessed in the hall and in the field,
Under the mantle as the shield.
Avenger of thy country's shame,
Restorer of her injured name,
Blessed in thy scepter and thy sword,
De Bruce, fair Scotland's rightful lord,
Blessed in thy deeds and in thy fame,
What lengthened honors wait thy name!
In distant ages, sire to son
Shall tell the tale of freedom won,

5

And teach his infants, in the use
Of earliest speech, to falter Bruce.
Go then, triumphant! sweep along
Thy course, the theme of many a song!
The power, whose dictates swell my breast,
Hath blessed thee, and thou shalt be blessed!"

21. With the faithful islanders Bruce remained for some months, while his friends were making preparations for a rising upon the mainland. At last the time came, and Bruce, at the head of a little force, landed in the night and surprised and captured a castle held by the Lord of Lorn. Holding this as a basis of operations, the king and his principal followers, Douglas and Randolph, went out in different directions to arouse the people against their English oppressors, and to raise forces of sufficient strength to risk their cause in battle. This was a matter of great hazard, as every movement of the Scotch was closely watched by the enemy, and, when any one was suspected of opposing the English rule, he was at once imprisoned and probably executed. The patriots were obliged to move with great caution, and often to secrete themselves in the fastnesses of the mountains or in the lonely huts of the peasants. Blood-hounds were employed to track the fugitives, and it is related that Lorn at one time followed Bruce with a blood-hound that had once been his own. The king, seeing that he was followed by a large body of soldiers, divided his men into three separate parties, hoping to throw the hound off the track. The blood-hound, when he came to the point of separation, would not even notice the two other divisions, but followed that of the king. Finding his last expedient had failed, Bruce ordered his whole party to disperse, keeping with him only his foster-brother as an

attendant. When Lorn discovered the party had broken up, he sent five of his men who were speedy on foot to follow the king and put him to death. They ran so fast that they soon gained sight of Bruce and his companion. The two turned upon the five men of Lorn, who came up one by one, exhausted with running, and put them all to death.

22. By this time Bruce was much fatigued, but he dared not stop to rest, for he could hear every moment the deep bay of the hound. At length they came to a wood through which ran a small stream of water. Into the stream they waded and followed it for a long distance; the blood-hound followed the track to the water, but he could trace the scent no farther, and Lorn gave up the chase. But Bruce's adventures were not at an end. After resting themselves in the woods, the two set out to find some human habitation, or to fall in with some party of their friends. In the midst of the forest they met three men who looked like ruffians. "They were well armed, and one of them bore a sheep on his back, which it seemed he had just stolen. They saluted the king civilly, and he, replying to their salutation, asked them where they were going. The men answered that they were seeking for Robert Bruce, for they intended to join him. The king answered that, if they would go with him, he would conduct them where they could find the Scottish king. Then the man who had spoken changed color, and Bruce, who looked sharply at him, began to suspect that the ruffian guessed who he was, and that he and his companions had some design against his person, in order to gain the reward which had been offered for his life.

23. "So he said to them, 'My good friends, as we are not well acquainted with each other, you must go before us,

and we will follow near to you.' 'You have no occasion to suspect any harm from us,' said the man. 'Neither do I suspect any,' said Bruce, 'but this is the way in which I choose to travel.'

24. "The men did as he commanded, and thus they traveled till they came to a waste and ruinous cottage, where the men proposed to dress down part of the sheep which they were carrying. The king was glad to hear of food, but he insisted that two fires should be kindled, one for himself and foster-brother at one end of the cottage, the other at the other end for the three companions. The men did as he desired. They broiled a quarter of the mutton for themselves, and gave another to the king and his attendant. They were obliged to eat it without bread or salt; but, as they were very hungry, they were glad to get food in any shape, and partook of it heartily.

25. "Then so heavy a drowsiness fell on King Robert that he greatly desired to sleep. But, first, he desired his foster-brother to watch as he slept, for he had great suspicion of his new acquaintances. His foster-brother promised to keep awake, and did his best to so keep his word. But the king had not been long asleep ere his foster-brother fell into a deep slumber also, for he had undergone as much fatigue as the king.

26. "When the three villains saw the king and his attendant were asleep, they made signs to each other, and, rising up, at once drew their swords with the purpose to kill them both. But the king slept but lightly, and, as little noise as the traitors made in rising, he was awakened by it, and, starting up, drew his sword and went to meet them. At the same moment he pushed his foster-brother with his foot to awaken him, and he started up; but, ere he got his eyes cleared to see what was about him, one of the ruffians that were advancing to slay the king killed him

with the stroke of a sword. The king was now alone—one man against three, and in the greatest danger of his life; but his amazing strength, and the good armor which he wore, freed him from this great danger, and he killed the men one by one.

27. "King Robert was now alone, and he left the cottage very sorrowful for the death of his foster-brother, and took himself in the direction toward where he had directed his men to ensemble after their dispersion. It was now near night, and, the place of meeting being a farm-house, he went boldly into it, where he found the mistress, an old true-hearted Scotchwoman, sitting alone. Upon seeing a stranger enter, she asked him who and what he was. The king answered that he was a traveler, who was journeying through the country. 'All travelers,' answered the good woman, 'are welcome here for the sake of one.' 'And who is that one,' said the king, 'for whose sake you make all travelers welcome?' 'It is our lawful King Robert the Bruce,' answered the mistress, 'who is the rightful lord of this country; and, although he is now pursued and hunted after with hounds and horns, I hope to live to see him king over all Scotland.'

28. "'Since you love him so well, dame,' said the king, 'know that you see him before you. I am Robert the Bruce.' 'You!' said the good woman in great surprise; 'and wherefore are you thus alone? Where are all your men?' 'I have none with me at this moment,' answered the Bruce, 'and therefore I must travel alone.' 'But that shall not be,' said the brave old dame, 'for I have two stout sons, gallant and trusty men, who shall be your servants for life and death!' So she brought her sons, and, though she well knew the danger to which she exposed them, she made them swear fealty to the king; and they afterward became high officers in his service.

29. "Now the loyal old woman was getting everything ready for the king's supper, when suddenly there was a trampling of horse heard around the house. They thought it must be some of the English or John of Lorn's men, and the good wife called upon her sons to fight to the last for King Robert. But, shortly after, the voices of James of Douglas and of Edward Bruce, the king's brother, were heard, who had come with a hundred and fifty horsemen to this farm-house, according to the instructions of the king when they parted.

30. "Robert the Bruce was right joyful to meet his brother and faithful friend Lord James, and had no sooner found himself at the head of such a considerable body of followers, than, forgetting hunger and weariness, he began to inquire where the enemy who had pursued him so long had taken up their quarters; 'for,' said he, 'as they must suppose we are totally scattered and fled, it is likely they will think themselves quite secure, and disperse themselves into distant quarters, and keep careless watch.'

31. "'That is very true,' answered James of Douglas; 'for I passed a village where there are two hundred of them quartered who had placed no sentinels; and, if you have a mind to make haste, we may surprise them this very night.' Then there was nothing but mount and ride; and, as the Scots came by surprise on the body of the English whom Douglas had mentioned, and rushed suddenly into the village where they were quartered, they easily dispersed and cut them to pieces; thus doing their pursuers more injury than they themselves had received during the long and severe pursuit of the preceding day."

32. On another occasion Bruce, with sixty men, was wandering in the county of Galloway, awaiting the gathering of forces. Now the people of Galloway are mostly

friendly to the Lord of Lorn, and a large number of them collected, determined to capture him. They felt sure of the success of their enterprise, as they had a blood-hound to track the king, and had such superior numbers.

33. "Now Bruce, who was always watchful and vigilant, had received some information of this party to come upon him suddenly in the night. Accordingly, he quartered his party of sixty men on the farther side of a deep and swift-running river, that had very steep and rocky banks. There was but one ford by which this river could be crossed in the neighborhood, and that ford was deep and narrow, so that two men could scarcely get through abreast; the bank on which they were to land on the other side was steep, and the path that led upward from the water's edge extremely narrow and difficult.

34. "Bruce caused his men to lie down and sleep, at a place about half a mile distant from the river, while he, with two attendants, went down to watch the ford, and thinking how easily the enemy might be kept from passing there, providing it was bravely defended—when he heard the distant baying of a hound, which was always coming nearer and nearer. This was the blood-hound which was tracing the king's steps to the ford where he had crossed, and the two hundred Galloway men were along with the animal and guided by it. Bruce thought of going back to awaken his men; but then he thought it might be some shepherd's dog. 'My men,' said he, 'are sorely tired; I will not disturb them by the barking of a cur till I know something more of the matter.'

35. "So he stood and listened; and, by and by, as the cry of the hound came nearer, he began to hear the trampling of horses, and the voices of men, and the ringing and clattering of armor; and then he was sure the enemy were coming to the river-side. Then the king thought,

'If I go back to give my men the alarm, these Galloway men will get through the ford without opposition, and that would be a pity, since it is a place so advantageous to make a defense against them.' So he looked again at the steep path and the deep river, and he thought it gave him so much advantage that he could defend the passage with his own hand until his men came to assist him. His armor was so good and strong that he had no fears of their arrows, and therefore the combat was not so very unequal as it must have otherwise seemed. He therefore sent his followers to waken his men, and remained alone on the bank of the river.

36. "In the meanwhile the noise and the trampling of the horses increased, and, the moon being bright, Bruce saw the glancing arms of about two hundred men, who came down to the opposite bank of the river. The men of Galloway, on their part, saw but one solitary figure guarding the ford, and the foremost of them plunged into the river without minding him. Bruce, who stood high above them on the bank where they were to land, killed the foremost man with a thrust of his long spear, and with a second thrust stabbed the horse, which fell down, kicking and plunging in his agonies, on the narrow path, and so preventing the others from getting out of the river. In the confusion five or six of the enemy were slain, or, having been borne down the current, were drowned in the river. The rest were terrified, and drew back.

37. "But, when they looked again and saw only one man, they themselves being so many, they cried out that their honor would be lost forever if they did not force their way; and encouraged each other with loud cries to plunge in and assault him. But by this time the king's soldiers came up to his assistance, and the Galloway men retreated and gave up their enterprise."

38. These successes of Bruce inspired great confidence, and he soon found himself at the head of a formidable force. With this he marched up and down the country, and compelled the English to keep strictly within their castles and fortified places; and even several of these were captured. King Edward I, of England, heard of these successes of Bruce with astonishment and rage. Though old and sorely diseased, he raised a large army and marched for the north; but he had scarcely crossed the Scottish border when his physician informed him that he had but a few hours to live. He immediately called his son to his bed-side, and made him swear that he would push forward this expedition against the Bruce; and he died cursing the whole Scotch people. He even gave direction that his body should be boiled, and that his bones, wrapped in a bull's hide, should be carried at the head of the army as often as the Scots attempted to recover their freedom.

39. Edward II was a weak prince, neither so wise nor so brave as his father. He marched a little way on to Scotland, but, having no great liking for war, he turned and marched back into England. He disregarded his father's injunction about the disposition of his bones, but took them back to London, and deposited them in Westminster Abbey.

40. From this time the cause of Bruce was a succession of victories. During the winter and spring one English fortress after another surrendered, until there only remained the strong castle of Stirling held by the English power. This castle was besieged, and Sir Philip Mowbray, the commander, agreed to surrender it if it was not reinforced by the English before midsummer. Then came a cessation of hostilities, and a period of rest for the Scots. King Edward had made no arrangement to again interfere in Scottish affairs. But now, when Sir Philip Mowbray,

the governor of Stirling, came to London to tell the king that Stirling, the last Scottish town of importance which remained in possession of the English, was to be surrendered if it were not relieved by force of arms before midsummer, then all the English nobles called out, it would be a sin and shame to permit the fair conquest which Edward I had made to be forfeited to the Scots for want of fighting. It was, therefore, resolved that the king should go himself to Scotland with as great forces as he could possibly muster.

41. King Edward II, therefore, assembled one of the greatest armies which a king of England ever commanded. There were troops brought from all his dominions. Many brave soldiers from the French provinces which the king of England enjoyed in France; many Irish, many Welsh, and all the great English nobles and barons, with their followers, were assembled in one great army. The number was not less than one hundred thousand men.

42. King Robert the Bruce summoned all his nobles and barons to join him, when he heard of the great preparation which the king of England was making. They were not so numerous as the English by many thousand men. In fact, his whole army did not very much exceed thirty thousand men, and they were much worse armed than the wealthy Englishmen; but then Robert, who was at their head, was one of the most expert generals of the time, and the officers he had under him were his brother Edward, his nephew Randolph, his faithful follower the Douglas, and other brave and experienced leaders, who commanded the same men that had been accustomed to fight and gain victories under every disadvantage of situation and numbers.

43. The king, on his part, studied how he might supply, by address and stratagem, what he wanted in num-

bers and strength. He knew the superiority of the English both in their heavy-armed cavalry, which were much better mounted and armed than those of the Scots, and in the archery, in which art the English were better than any people in the world. Both these advantages he resolved to provide against. With this purpose, Bruce led his army down into a plain, near Stirling, called the Park, near which, and beneath it, the English army must needs pass through a boggy country, broken with water-courses, while the Scots occupied hard, dry ground. He then caused all the hard ground upon the front of his line of battle, where cavalry were likely to act, to be dug full of holes, about as deep as a man's knee. They were filled with light brushwood, and the turf was laid on the top, so that it appeared a plain field, while in reality it was all as full of these pits as a honeycomb is of holes. He also, it is said, caused steel spikes, called calthrops, to be scattered up and down in the plain, where the English cavalry were most likely to advance, trusting to lame and destroy their horses.

44. When his army was drawn, the line stretched north and south. On the south it was terminated by the banks of the brook called Bannockburn, which are so rocky that no troops could come on them there. On the left the Scottish line extended near to the town of Stirling. Bruce reviewed his troops very carefully; all the useless servants and drivers of carts, and such like, of whom there were very many, he ordered to go behind a height called the Gillies' Hill—that is, the Servants' Hill. He then spoke to the soldiers, and expressed his determination to gain the victory or to lose his life on the field of battle. He desired that all those who did not propose to fight to the last would leave the field before the battle began, and that none would remain except those who were

determined to take the issue of victory or death, as God should send it.

45. Burns has expressed Bruce's sentiments in his fiery poem.

BRUCE'S ADDRESS.

46. Scots who have with Wallace bled,
Scots whom Bruce has often led,
Welcome to your gory bed
Or to victory!
Now's the day, and now's the hour;
See the front of battle lower;
See approach proud Edward's power,
Chains, and slavery!

47. Who would be a traitor knave,
Who would fill a coward's grave,
Who so base as be a slave,
Let him turn and flee!
Who for Scotland's king and law,
Freedom's sword will strongly draw,
Freeman stand, or freeman fa',
Let him follow me!

48. By oppressions, woes, and pains,
By our sons in servile chains,
We will drain our dearest veins,
But they shall be free!
Lay the proud usurper low!
Tyrants fall in every foe—
Liberty at every blow;
Let us do or die!

49. When the main body of his army was thus placed in order, the king posted Randolph, with a body of horse,

near to the church of St. Mirau's, commanding him to use the utmost diligence to prevent any succorers from being thrown into Stirling Castle. He then dismissed James of Douglas and Sir Robert Keith, the marshal of the Scottish army, in order that they might survey, as nearly as they could, the English force, which was now approaching from Falkirk. They returned with information that the approach of that vast host was one of the most beautiful and terrible sights which could be seen; that the whole country seemed covered with men-at-arms on horse and foot; that the number of standard banners and pennants made so gallant a show, that the bravest and most numerous host in Christendom might be alarmed to see King Edward moving against them.

50. It was upon the 23d of June, 1314, that the King of Scotland heard the news that the English army were approaching Stirling. He drew out his army, therefore, in the order which he had before resolved upon. After a short time, Bruce, who was looking out anxiously for the enemy, saw a body of English cavalry trying to get into Stirling from the eastward. This was the Lord Clifford, who, with a chosen body of eight hundred horse, had been detached to relieve the castle.

51. "See, Randolph," said the king to his nephew, "there is a rose fallen from your chaplet." By this he meant that Randolph has lost some honor by suffering the enemy to pass where he had been commanded to follow them. Randolph made no reply, but rushed against Clifford with little more than half his number. The Scots were on foot. The English turned to charge them with their lances, and Randolph drew up his men in close order to receive them. He seemed to be in so much danger that Douglas asked leave of the king to go and assist him. The king refused permission.

52. "Let Randolph," he said, "redeem his own fault. I can not break the order of battle for his sake." Still the danger appeared greater, and the English horse seemed entirely to encompass the small handful of Scottish infantry. "To please you," said Douglas to the king, "my heart will not suffer me to stand idle and see Randolph perish. I must go to his assistance." He rode off accordingly, but long before they had reached the place of combat they saw the English horses galloping off, many with their empty saddles.

53. "Halt!" said Douglas to his men. "Randolph has gained the day. Since we were not soon enough to help him in the battle, do not let us lessen his glory by approaching the field." Now, that was nobly done, especially as Douglas and Randolph were always contending which should rise highest in the good opinion of the king and the nation.

54. The van of the English army now came in sight, and a number of their bravest knights drew near to see what the Scottish were doing. They saw King Robert dressed in his armor, and distinguished by a gold crown which he wore over his helmet. He was not mounted on his great war horse, because he did not expect to fight that evening. But he rode on a little pony up and down the ranks of his army, putting his men in order, and carried in his hand a short battle-axe made of steel. When the king saw the English horsemen draw near, he advanced a little before his own men, that he might look at them more nearly.

55. There was a knight among the English called Sir Henry de Bohun, who thought this would be a good opportunity to gain great fame to himself and put an end to the war by killing King Robert. The king being poorly mounted, and having no lance, Bohun galloped

on him suddenly and furiously, thinking, with his long spear and his big strong horse, easily to bear him down to the ground. King Robert saw him and permitted him to come very near, then suddenly turned his pony a little to one side, so that Sir Henry missed him with the lance point, and was in the act of being carried past him by the career of his horse. But as he passed, King Robert rose up in his stirrups and struck Sir Henry on the head with his battle-axe so terrible a blow that it broke to pieces his iron helmet, as if it had been a nutshell, and hurled him from his saddle. He was dead before he reached the ground. This gallant action was blamed by the Scottish leaders, who thought Bruce ought not to have exposed himself to so much danger when the safety of the whole army depended on him. The king only kept looking at his weapon, which was injured by the force of the blow, and said, "I have broken my good battle-axe." This is the way Scott describes this incident in the "Lord of the Isles":

56. O gay yet fearful to behold,
Flashing with steel and rough with gold,
And bristled o'er with balls and spears,
With plumes and pennons waving fair,
Was that bright battle front! for there
Rode England's king and peers.

57. And who that saw that monarch ride,
His kingdom battling by his side,
Could then his direful doom foretell;
Fair was his seat in knightly selle,
And in his sprightly eye was set
Some sparks of the Plantagenet.

Though bright and wandering was his glance,
It flashed at sight of shield and lance.
"Knowest thou," he said, "De Argentine,
Yon knight who marshals thus their line?"

58. "The tokens on his helmet tell
The Bruce, my liege; I know him well."
"And shall the audacious traitor brave
The presence where our banners wave?"
"So please my liege," said Argentine,
"Were he but horsed on steed like mine,
To give him fair and knightly chance,
I would adventure forth my lance."

59. "In battle-day," the king replied,
"Nice tourney rules are set aside;
Still must the rebel dare our wrath!
Set on him—sweep him from our path!"
And, at King Edward's signal, soon
Dashed from the ranks Sir Edward Bohun!

60. Of Hereford's high blood he came,
A race renowned for knightly fame;
He burned before his monarch's eye
To do some deed of chivalry.
He spurred his steed, he couched his lance,
And darted on the Bruce at once.
As motionless as rocks, that bide
The wrath of the advancing tide,
The Bruce stood fast; each breast beat high,
And dazzled was each gazing eye;
The heart had hardly time to think,
The eyelid scarce had time to wink,

While on the king, like flash of flame,
Spurred to full speed, the war-horse came!
The partridge may the falcon mock,
If that slight palfrey stand the shock;
But, swerving from the knight's career,
Just as they met, Bruce shunned the spear;
Onward the baffled warrior bore
His course—but soon his course was o'er!
High in his stirrups stood the king,
And gave his battle-axe the swing.
Right on De Bohun, the whiles he passed,
Fell that stern dint—the first—the last!
Such strength upon the blow was put,
The helmet crushed like hazel-nut,
The axe-shaft, with its brazen clasp,
Was shivered to the gauntlet grasp.
Springs from the blow the startled horse,
Drops on the plain the lifeless corse;
First of that fatal field, how soon,
How sudden fell the fierce De Bohun!

61. One pitying glance the monarch shed
Where on the field his foe lay dead;
Then gently turned his palfrey's head,
And, pacing back his sober way,
Slowly he gained his own array.
There round their king the leaders crowd
And blame his recklessness aloud,
That risked 'gainst each adventurous spear
A life so valued and so dear.
His broken weapon's shaft surveyed
The king, and careless answer made:
"My loss must pay my folly's tax—
I've broke my trusty battle-axe."

62. The next morning, being the 24th of June, at break of day the battle began in terrible earnest. The English as they advanced saw the Scots getting into line. The Abbot of Inchaffray walked through their ranks barefooted, and exhorted them to fight for their freedom. They kneeled down as he passed, and prayed to heaven for victory. King Edward, who saw this, called out: "They kneel down; they are asking forgiveness." "Yes," said a celebrated English baron, called Ingelram de Umphraville, "but they ask it from God, not from us; these men will conquer, or die upon the field." The English king ordered his men to begin the battle. The archers then bent their bows, and began to shoot so closely together that the arrows fell like flakes of snow on a Christmas-day.

63. Upon the right, behind the wood,
Each by his steed, dismounted, stood
The Scottish chivalry;
With foot in stirrup, hand on mane,
Fierce Edward Bruce can scarce restrain
His own keen heart, his eager train,
Until the archers gain the plain;
Then "Mount ye gallants free!"
He cried; and, vaulting from the ground,
His saddle every horseman found.
On high their glittering crests they toss,
As springs the wild-fire from the moss;
The shield hangs down on every breast,
Each ready lance is in the rest,
And loud shouts Edward Bruce:
"Forth, marshal! on the peasant foe!
We'll tame the terrors of their bow,
And cut the bow-string loose!"

64. Then spurs were dashed in chargers' flanks,
They rushed among the archer ranks.
No spears were there the shock to let,
No stakes to turn the charge were set,
And how shall yeoman's armor slight,
Stand the long lance and mace of might?
Or what may their short swords avail,
'Gainst barbèd horse and shirt of mail?
Amid their ranks the chargers spring,
High o'er their heads the weapons swing,
And shriek and groan and vengeful shout
Give note of triumph and of rout!
Awhile, with stubborn hardihood,
Their English hearts the strife made good;
Borne down at length on every side,
Compelled to flight, they scatter wide.
Let stags of Sherwood leap for glee,
And bound the deer of Dallorn-Lee!
The broken bows of Bannock's shore
Shall in the greenwood ring no more!
Round Wakefield's merry May-pole now,
The maids may twine the summer bough,
May northward look with longing glance
For those that went to lead the dance,
For the blithe archers look in vain!
Broken, dispersed, in flight o'erta'en,
Pierced through, trod down, by thousands slain,
They cumber Bannock's bloody plain!

65. The fine English cavalry then advanced to support their archers, and to attack the Scottish line. But coming over the ground which was dug full of pits the horses fell into these holes, and the riders lay tumbling about, without any means of defense, and unable to rise, from

the weight of their armor. The Englishmen began to fall into general disorder; and the Scottish king, bringing up more of his forces, attacked and pressed them still more closely.

66. On a sudden an event happened which decided the victory. The servants and attendants on the Scottish camp had been sent behind the army to a place called Gillies' Hill; but now, when they saw that their masters were like to gain the day, they rushed from their place of concealment with such weapons as they could get, that they might have their share in the victory and in the spoil. The English, seeing them come suddenly over the hill, mistook the disorderly rabble for a new army coming up to sustain the Scots; and, losing all heart, began to shift every man for himself. Edward himself left the field as fast as he could ride, and was closely pursued by Douglas, with a party of horse, who followed him as far as Dunbar, where the English had still a friend in the governor, Patrick, Earl of Mans. The earl received Edward in his forlorn condition, and furnished him with a fishing skiff, or small ship, in which he escaped to England, having entirely lost his fine army, and a great number of his bravest nobles.

67. The English never before or afterward lost so dreadful a battle as that of Bannockburn, nor did the Scots ever gain one of the same importance. Many of the best and bravest of the English nobility and gentry lay dead on the field; a great many more were made prisoners, and the whole of King Edward's immense army was dispersed or destroyed.

68. Thus did Robert Bruce arise from the condition of an exile, hunted with blood-hounds like a stag or beast of prey, to the rank of an independent sovereign, universally acknowledged to be one of the wisest and bravest

kings who then lived. The nation of Scotland was also raised once more from the state of a distressed and conquered province to that of a free and independent state, governed by its own laws, and subject to its own princes; and although the country was, after the Bruce's death, often subjected to great loss and distress, both by the hostility of the English and by the unhappy civil wars among the Scots themselves, yet they never afterward lost the freedom for which Wallace had laid down his life, and which King Robert had recovered no less by his wisdom than by his weapons. And therefore most just it is that, while the country of Scotland retains any recollection of its history, the memory of these brave warriors and faithful patriots ought to be remembered with honor and gratitude.

69. In 1328, fourteen years after the battle of Bannockburn, peace was concluded between England and Scotland, in which the English surrendered all pretension to the Scottish crown. King Robert was now fifty-four years old, and he prepared to enter upon a crusade in accordance with his vow, and in expiation of his offense of slaying the Red Comyn. But, being smitten with a fatal disease, he directed Lord James, of Douglas, upon his death, to take his heart and carry it to Palestine, in fulfillment of his vow. Douglas accepted the sacred trust, and encased the heart in silver, and hung it about his neck. On his way to the Holy Land he turned aside to help the Spaniard in a campaign against the Moors. In one battle, being sorely beset, he flung the heart of Bruce into the midst of the enemy, and followed it up with the war-cry of the Douglas, which had so often cheered to victory among his native hills. At every step a Moslem bit the dust until he reached the spot where his master's heart had fell. Here he was slain by the numbers which pressed

in on every side, and he was found with his body still in the attitude of guarding the heart. The body of Lord James, together with the heart, were returned to Scotland. The precious relic—the last that remained of the Bruce, the greatest of Scottish kings—was deposited in Melrose Abbey, where it remains to-day a sacred shrine for every Scotchman, and for every lover of liberty. Rarely in the history of man has the prediction of the old abbot been so literally fulfilled:

"I bless thee, and thou shalt be blest!"

CHAPTER V.

COLUMBUS AND THE NEW WORLD.

THE TIME.

1. Columbus lived in a stirring age. Everywhere light was breaking in after centuries of darkness, and all Europe was restless with suggestions and beginnings of new life. Great men were plenty; rulers, like the Medici of Florence; artists, like Raphael and Angelo; preachers, like Savonarola, whose fiery prophecies brought him to fiery death; reformers, chief among them Luther, just beginning to think the thoughts that later set the world agog. Great inventions were spreading; gunpowder, invented before, now becoming terribly effective through the improvement in guns; printing, suddenly opening knowledge to every class; the little compass, with which mariners were just beginning to trust themselves boldly on the seas, in spite of the popular impression that it was a sort of infernal machine presided over by the devil himself.

2. And to this age had been bequeathed the fascinating stories of Sir John Mandeville and Marco Polo, stories to make every boy crazy to be off to seek his fortune. From their travels in Asia these men had brought back the most remarkable accounts of these eastern lands. "A country was there," they said, "called

SHIPS OF COLUMBUS

Cathay, bordering on the sea. It was ruled by an emperor, the Kubla Khan, or Great Khan, who lighted his bedroom with a bright jewel half a foot long, set upon golden pillars, and decorated his walls with wrought gold and hundreds of precious stones. The rivers of the land were crossed by marble bridges, and the houses were roofed and paved with gold. The seas were full of islands where spices grew and countless strange creatures lived: one-eyed men; men with a lip long enough to cover their whole face; men with only one foot, but that so large that they held it over them like an umbrella when they lay down in the sun to rest; two-headed men and men with no heads at all; men whose only food was snakes, and others whose favorite beverage was human blood; dragons and unicorns; woolly hens and sheep that grew on trees; and in one island a valley where only devils dwelt. But there were besides great hills of gold, cities with towers of silver and gold, precious stones of all kinds, and rose-tinted pearls, big and round."

3. There was trade between Europe and certain parts of Asia which they called the Indies, and reached by going east and south by land; but this marvelous country of the Grand Khan lay beyond, and its riches remained a golden dream, known only by the travelers' reports. That was what was known of Asia. Of Africa, even less; for fifty years before Columbus was born only a strip across the northern part of it was known, and south of that lay "nothing," said the people. And of America, our wide-stretching America, they never dreamed.

4. Some fifty years before the birth of Columbus, Prince Henry of Portugal, studying the matter, came to the conclusion that the world did not necessarily end at "Cape Nothing," on the African coast, as people said, but perhaps extended a long way farther; and, having an

abundance of time and money, he began to send out ships to sail along beyond the cape and see what they could find. And they found a long, long coast. Year after year, until the prince was a gray-haired old man, he sent out vessel after vessel; and, though often storm-driven and wrecked, and unsuccessful, they many times came back with accounts of new discoveries. One by one they brought the numerous islands lying off the northwest coast of Africa to the notice of the people of Europe. And after they once got past that mysterious "Cape Nothing," they sailed along the coast, going farther and farther on successive voyages, until, in 1487, long after Prince Henry's death, and just before Columbus's great voyage, the most southern point was rounded, the African continent was known, and the long-sought water-way to the Indies was established.

THE IDEA.

5. As to the date of Columbus's birth, historians can not agree within some ten years. It was doubtless somewhere between 1435 and 1446. They also give different accounts as to his birthplace; but it seems most probable that he was born in Genoa, on the Mediterranean, the son of a wool-carder, and that he went to school in Pavia. At fourteen he became a sailor.

6. Up and down the seas, first in the sunny Mediterranean, later along the stormy Atlantic coast, sailed the lad, the young man, in the small sailing vessels of the time, and learned well the ocean which he afterward so boldly trusted.

7. He was a daring, quick-witted, handsome, bronzed young man when he went to Lisbon, where his brother Bartholomew was established as a cosmographer, making

View of Genoa.

charts for seamen; and with all his enthusiasm for his sea-faring life, he had enough interest in ordinary pursuits to fall in love most romantically. It happened on account of his being so regular at church. Every day he must attend service, and every day to church came Donna Philippa Palestrello, who lived in a convent near by. Across the seats flitted involuntary glances between the cloistered maiden and the handsome brown sailor—with a dimple in his chin, some pictures have him; something besides prayers were read between the lines of the prayer-book, and the marriage which closed this churchly wooing proved the wisdom of both parties.

8. Philippa's father had been one of Prince Henry's famous seamen and the governor of Porto Santo, one of the new-found islands; and after his marriage, Columbus lived sometimes at Porto Santo, sometimes at Lisbon, and much of the time on the sea. He sailed south along the African coast to Guinea; north he sailed to England, and farther on to Iceland. Wherever ships could go, there went he, intent on learning all there was to know of the world he lived in. He read eagerly all that was written about the earth's shape and size. The modern science of his time he well understood. He pored over the maps of the ancient geographer Ptolemy, over the maps of Cosmas, a later geographer, over Palestrello's charts, given him by Philippa's mother.

9. Ptolemy said the world is round, but Cosmas, whom good Christians were bound to believe, since he founded his science on the Bible, said it is flat, with a wall around it to hold up the sky—very probable, certainly. But that notion of the ancients that the world is "round like a ball" had been caught up and believed by a handful of men scattered sparsely down through the centuries, and of late had gained, among advanced scientists, more of a

following than ever. And Columbus, who, with all his enthusiasm for adventure and his reverence for religion and the church, had a clear, unbiassed, scientific head, mentally turned his back upon Cosmas, and clasped hands with the ancients and the wisest scientists of his own day.

10. The north was known, the south was fast becoming so, the east had been penetrated, but the west was unexplored. Stretching along from Thule, the distant Iceland, to the southern part of the great African continent, thousands of miles, lay the "Sea of Darkness," as the people called it. What lay beyond? The question had been asked before, times enough; times enough answered for any reasonable man. "Hell was there," said one superstition, "Haven't you seen the flames at sunset-time?" "A sea thick like paste, in which no ships can sail," said another. "Darkness," said another, "thick darkness, the blackness of nothing, and the end of all created things!"

11. There *was* a legend that over there beyond was Paradise, and St. Brandan, wandering about the seas, had reached it. The ancients told of an island Atlantis over there somewhere in the West, and one of them had said: "In the last days an age will come when ocean shall loose the chains of things; a wonderful country will be discovered, and Tiphis shall make known new worlds, nor shall Thule be the end of the earth."

12. Ah, to be the discoverer of Atlantis or Paradise! "But, if the world is round," said Columbus, "it is not hell that lies beyond that stormy sea. Over there *must* lie the eastern strand of Asia, the Cathay of Marco Polo, the land of the Kubla Khan, and Cipango, the great island beyond it." "Nonsense!" said the neighbors; "the world isn't round—can't you *see* it is flat? And Cosmas Indicopleustes, who lived hundreds of years before you were born, says it is flat; and he got it from the Bible.

You're no good Christian to be taking up with such heathenish notions!" Thought Columbus, "I will write to Paolo Toscanelli, at Florence, and see what he will say."

13. So Columbus wrote, and Toscanelli, the wise scientist, answered that the idea of sailing west was good and feasible; and with the letter came a map, on which Asia and the great island Cipango were laid down opposite Europe, with the Atlantic between, exactly as Columbus imagined it. Toscanelli said it was easy enough: "You may be certain of meeting with extensive kingdoms, populous cities, and rich provinces, abounding in all sorts of precious stones; and your visit will cause great rejoicing to the king and princes of those distant lands, besides opening a way for communication between them and the Christians, and the instruction of them in the Catholic region and the arts we possess." It was 1474 when this encouragement came, and from this time all the sailor's thoughts and plans turn toward the west.

14. The life at home between his voyages, whether spent with his brother, the cosmographer, at Lisbon, or with his wife and sailor brother-in-law, on the Porto Santo island, was hardly less nautical than the voyages themselves. Porto Santo was in line with the ship-routes to and from Spain and all the new-found African coast and islands; and the family there, with the men sailors and geographers, and the women, wives and daughters of sailors and geographers, lived in the bracing salt sea-air, full of the tingle of adventure.

15. Wild stories tell the sailors, coming and going, whom one can scarce contradict for lack of certain knowledge; and is it not an age of wonders in real life? And the round earth, the round earth—*is* it round? And the empire of the Grand Khan just over the western water there—not far! The sailors said that on the shores of one

of the islands two dead men of strange appearance had been washed in from the west. The sailors said they had picked up curiously-carved sticks drifting from the west. Pedro Correa himself, Columbus's brother-in-law, and a man to be trusted, had found one floating from the west. And there was a legend of the sight of land lying like a faint cloud along that western horizon.

16. "The world *is* round," said Columbus. "It is not very large" (he thought it much smaller than it is), "and opposite us across that sea lies Asia; and to Asia by way of that sea I will go. There, in the west, lies my duty to God and man; I will carry salvation to the heathen, and bring back gold for the Christians. From the 'Occident to the Orient' a path I will find through the waters."

THE WAITING.

17. Such a venture as Columbus proposed could scarcely be carried out at that time except by the help of kings, so to the kings went Columbus.

18. Naturally, Portugal, with her proved interest in discovery, came first in his thought; and before Portugal's king he laid his project. The king should fit him out with vessels and men, and with them Columbus would sail to the Indies, not by the route around Africa, which the Portuguese had so long been seeking, but by a nearer way—straight across the Atlantic. Think of the untold wealth from the empire of the khan rolling in to Portugal if this connection could be established! And think of converting those heathen to our blessed mother church! It was worth thinking about, and the king called a council of his wise men to consider the startling idea. Not long were the wise men in wisely deciding that the plan was the wild scheme of an adventurer, likely to come to

no good whatever; and when the king, hardly satisfied, laid it before another council, they, too, wisely declared it ridiculous.

19. O ye owlish dignitaries! Still, the king was not convinced. "We have discovered much by daring adventure, why not more?" "Stick to the coast, and don't go sailing straight away from all known land into waters unknown and mysterious," said the wise men. "But if the unknown waters bring us to the riches of Cathay?" said the king. "That's the extravagant dream of a visionary; it contains no truth and much danger," said the wise men. "Try it yourself, and see. Unbeknown to this Columbus, just send out a ship of your own to the west, and let them come back and tell us what they find."

20. It was a most underhand piece of business all around; but the king yielded and sent out a ship, which presently came back again with the report that there was no Cathay there, and they hadn't found any Cipango; it was all nonsense! And what they had met with was a big storm that scared them terribly. So Columbus retired, and left the king of Portugal to his brave sailors and wise councilors.

21. Next will come Spain, and meantime he will send his brother Bartholomew to present the plan at the English court.

22. The Spanish sovereigns, Ferdinand and Isabella, were down in Andalusia, that beautiful southern province of Spain, in the midst of a war with the Moors, who occupied certain portions of the land, and whom the Spaniards were trying to drive out. So, his wife being now dead, Columbus took his little boy Diego, and to Andalusia they went. They stopped at Palos by the sea, and from there set out on foot. The way was long, and Diego could not go far without getting very thirsty; and his farthest op-

ping at a great, dark, stone convent, called Maria de la Rabida, to get him a drink, the prior asked them in to rest a bit. As they talked, Columbus soon told of his great project, to sail to the Indies by way of the western sea.

23. The prior, in his long dark robe and shaved head, opened his eyes at this and wanted to hear more. "Novel project this," thought he; "very novel—most astonishing! I must have my friend, Dr. Fernandez, hear it." So a messenger was sent to Palos to fetch the doctor, and Columbus went over again the wonderful plan—just to sail west, not so very far, over the round earth, and reach the stately cities of Cathay, and convert the Grand Khan to the faith, and gather of the plentiful gold and jewels of that land. Little Diego stood by and listened with wide-open eyes, and the doctor pondered, while the prior gazed out from the western window upon the Atlantic, and Columbus bent eager eyes and flushed face over his chart.

24. "Why, it may be possible! Send for Martin Alonzo Pinzon. He is a seaman; let us see what he thinks!"

25. To Palos again goes the messenger, to the rich and influential citizen, Alonzo Pinzon, and tells him he is wanted at La Rabida. "Ah, Alonzo Pinzon!" greets him the prior, "come and hear what a man proposes to do; and a wise and courageous sailor he seems, though poor enough!" And a third time they bend over the charts there in the dark stone convent, and Alonzo Pinzon hears of the western route to India; and Diego gazes from one to the other, and hopes in his heart that his father will take him along—he wants to see the unicorns. Pinzon catches the idea with enthusiasm, promising to help Columbus with money and influence, and to go with him if he goes. The doctor, cogitating upon the statements

and arguments, concludes that they make quite a reasonable showing, and advises Columbus to go on.

26. The prior says: "Go at once to the court. Talavera, the queen's confessor, is a good friend of mine, and a letter of introduction to him will gain you access to the king and queen. They will surely help you." Diego clasps his hands. "Will you stay with me, Diego?" says the long-robed prior. "I'd rather go to court," says Diego. "Nay, my son," says Columbus, "if the good prior will keep you, I will leave you here while I go on my uncertain errand." So the little boy stands in the great stone doorway and watches his father out of sight toward Cordova.

27. At Cordova is nothing but excitement and confusion. The army is just starting upon a campaign against the Moors. Talavera is preoccupied, has his hands full of business, and can scarcely give Columbus time enough to state his errand. "Dear me, a new route to the Indies! But don't you see how busy we are with this war? It is probably all nonsense—sounds like it. The court in war-time can not waste precious hours over the consideration of such wild visions as this." So Columbus takes lodgings in Cordova, supports himself by chart-making, talks to everybody about the new route to Asia, and waits. Such a man with such a story is likely to gain some attention, and by and by he begins to have friends. Several of the important politicians come to know him, some are converts to his theory, and finally the grand cardinal himself procures him an audience with the king and queen.

28. Enthusiastically the "one-idea'd man" unfolds his theories to royalty. The land of the Grand Khan, with its untold treasure, the salvation of millions of souls in the Indies, are the vivid points. The earth is a sphere, and a ship may sail straight from Spain to Cipango, urges

this man of imagination and faith. The king was not slow to perceive the great advantages which success in such an enterprise would bring to the government that undertook it; but he must consult the wise men. Talavera should head a commission composed of the great men in the church, great men of science, and professors in the universities. Surely no man could ask for more. So to Salamanca, seat of the greatest Spanish university, Columbus went to convince the commission.

29. In the hall of the convent there was assembled the imposing company—shaved monks in gowns of black and gray, fashionably dressed men from the court in jaunty hats, cardinals in scarlet robes—all the dignity and learning of Spain, gathered and waiting for the man and his idea.

30. He stands before them with his charts, and explains his belief that the world is round, and that Asia stretches from the eastern boundary of Europe to a point something like four thousand miles from Spain. Hence Asia could be reached by sailing due west across the Atlantic. They had heard something of this before at Cordova, and here at Salamanca, before the commission was formally assembled, and they had their arguments ready.

31. You think the earth is round, and inhabited on the other side? Are you not aware that the holy fathers of the church have condemned this belief? Say the fathers, the Scriptures tell us all men are descended from Adam; but certainly no men descended from Adam live in such a region as this you speak of—the antipodes. Will you contradict the fathers? The Holy Scriptures, too, tell us expressly that the heavens are spread out like a tent, and how can that be true if the earth is not flat like the ground the tent stands on? This theory of yours looks heretical.

32. Columbus might well quake in his boots at the mention of heresy; for there was that new Inquisition just in fine running order, with its elaborate bone-breaking, flesh-pinching, thumb-screwing, hanging, burning, mangling system for heretics. What would become of the Idea if he should get passed over to that energetic institution?

33. "I am a true and loyal Catholic," he cries; "I wish to convert the Grand Khan's people to our blessed faith. I believe the Bible, and God himself sends me on this mission. But these words of the Scriptures are to be taken as a figure, not as literal facts of science." "Will this sailor teach us how to read the Scriptures!" growl the monks.

34. "Well, for argument, suppose this world is round, and you could sail west to the Indies. The voyage would take years, and you could not carry food enough to keep you from starving."

35. "But I believe it is only a voyage of four thousand miles, and can, with favoring winds, be accomplished in a short time," says Columbus, stating his scientific reasons for this belief. "Will this sailor teach us science!" growl the professors. "Well, all this *may* be true; but really, can you expect us to believe that there is a land beneath us where people walk with their feet *up*, and trees grow *down?*" Oh, foolish Columbus! What an absurd idea! "And, besides, if the signor should succeed in sailing down around the earth to this peculiar region, how does he propose to get back again? Will his ship sail up-hill?"

36. Oh, the nudgings and winks among the monks at this poser! And the professors smile triumphantly. "And, anyway, who are you, Signor Columbo, to set yourself up to know more than all the world beside?

Haven't men been sailing in all the seas ever since the time of Noah, and, if such a thing as this were possible, would not somebody have found it out long ago?" With sound science, reverent religion, enthusiastic imagination and faith, he answered them, this unknown sailor, and left them bewildered by his views and impressed by his personality. "Perhaps there is truth in the matter," said the monks of St. Stephen. They said they would think about it, and they did think about it, and it took them four years to think about it. Meantime they adjourned and went about their own affairs, and Columbus went back to court.

37. The campaign against the Moors began, and from that time to the end of those weary years Columbus followed the court from place to place, over the hills and valleys of beautiful Andalusia. Sometimes he made charts for his support, sometimes he fought in the battles, sometimes he talked with the courtiers, or begged audience with the king to urge him to a decision; but always was with him that one dream on which he was staking all his time and strength—the best years and the fullest power of his manhood—hope of his heart, purpose of his will, that one Idea possessing him in vivid, unwavering faith.

38. The queen was kind. His enthusiasm and sound judgment, his persistent faith in his idea, his dignity and strong determination, tempered by the most manly religion, made him friends even among his examiners at Salamanca; and so he hoped and waited. Think of it—four years of suspense on top of thirteen years of thought and study and investigation toward one end! And when at last Talavera assembled the wise men of the commission to announce the result of their long deliberation, they had come to this wise conclusion: that the whole

thing was foolish and impossible, unworthy of a great king's attention.

39. Better give it up, Cristoforo Colombo, and make charts for a living the rest of your days. No, says Colombo, that western ocean must be crossed. He turns to the powerful Spanish nobles. They are friendly, but hardly dare take up the project. He will go to France and present his case. But first to La Rabida to see Diego, a tall lad now. "What!" says the prior, "no success? Too bad, too bad! But Spain must not give the glory of this great undertaking to France. I know the queen, and I will write to her; I was her confessor once."

40. He wrote with such force that he was summoned to the queen at once, and his earnest pleading determined Isabella to send again for Columbus. But again disappointment came, for they took offense at Columbus's high demands and would not grant them. The Spanish sovereigns were to furnish the largest share of the equipment; he should be admiral of the seas, and he and his sons after him were to rule, under the king, the countries discovered, and share in all the profits of the enterprise. Bold demands from an adventurer! Seventeen years of waiting might have taught him common sense; but with his absurd faith and uncommon sense he would accept no other terms, and turned away again with his Idea and his determination.

41. "Too bad, too bad!" said St. Angel, the tax-collector; "*I* will plead with the queen. She must not let slip this chance of enriching the king—*and* converting the khan. I will myself lend the money necessary, if the king can't afford it." Said Isabella to St. Angel: "I think as you do. This is a wonderful plan. Let them say what they will, by my own right I am queen of Castile, as well as queen of Spain, and I pledge the crown of

Castile to raise for Cristoforo Columbo a suitable equipment to sail to the Indies by the west. Let him make his own terms."

42. At last the fretting applications, the repeated explanations, the harrowing suspense, the long restriction are over, and the strong wings of the sea-bird are free to bear away over the Atlantic.

THE VOYAGE.

43. At Palos, in Southern Spain, three small ships were provided. One, the Santa Maria, in which Columbus was to sail, was fully decked; the other two—the Pinta and the Niña—had decks and cabins only at the ends. As for crews, to secure them was no easy matter. Not many sailors cared to trust themselves upon that unknown "Sea of Darkness." Not many believed in this story of a western route to Asia.

44. A few, with visions of the Grand Khan's palaces and the marvelous sights of the East, would go for adventure's sake, and risk the mystery between. A few, thinking of the "great hills of gold," would risk the danger of tumbling into hell midway for the chance of getting safely across to the land of treasure. Alonzo Pinzon was on hand, as he had promised, and was given command of the Pinta, while the Niña was put in charge of his brother Vincent. Royal pardon for crimes and offenses was offered for any who would undertake this voyage, and so some jail-birds were added to the company. Queer stuff for such an undertaking! But beggars can not be choosers, and Cristoforo Colombo might be thankful that he could get anybody for his fool's errand!

45. On August 3, 1492, in the early morning, the three ships lay in Palos harbor, and down to Palos harbor

flock all the town to see them off for Cathay. Groups of trades-people shudder companionably over the vague terrors of the Atlantic, and chatter over the probabilities of the adventurers' return with untold wealth. Excited women—bareheaded, likely—gaze again upon the strong, controlled face of Columbus, and thank God for this missionary to the Grand Khan—only the dark sea will surely be his destruction before he gets there! Children wriggle through the throng and stare at the men who are soon to find out what becomes of the sun when it sets, and to know for themselves whether or no it hisses and makes the water boil. The sailors make their way toward the ships through a running fire of conversation and hand-clasps, culminating at the dock in general good-byes and the clinging embraces and sobs of daughters and sweethearts and wives. The Pinzons are there with their friends. Dr. Fernandez is going, too, and the prior of La Rabida, in his long robe, is exulting with him over this success. Diego, soon to go to court as page to the prince, is there to bid his father good-by.

46. Now all are on the docks ready to embark. A hundred and twenty men to brave the unknown terrors of that sea stretching before them! The prior steps gravely down among them, carrying the sacred host; kneeling before him, Columbus murmurs his last confession and receives the communion; and after him the Pinzons and the sailors reverently commune. The people are silent as the prior blesses the departing ones, and then the ships are manned, the sails spread, and Palos watches until they flutter, like white birds, out of sight—never to return! moan the daughters and the sweethearts and the wives; and the children, with wide dark eyes, whisper of the unicorns and dragons of the East.

47. Off at last! Oh, the exhilaration of it! Admiral

of three rickety ships and all the unknown seas; governor of a hundred disreputable sailors and the realms of Cathay!

48. They had not been out three days when the Pinta's rudder got out of order. That crew of the Pinta had been none too willing to start on this rash expedition, and Columbus had his suspicions that they put it out of order on purpose. Perhaps they did; anyway, the next day it was reported broken again, and Columbus pointed for one of the Canary Islands to get it mended. "We are going to Cathay by way of the western ocean," they said in reply to the islanders' questions. "Oh," said the islanders, "every year we can see land lying west of us, away off there. You will find it, though none of us have been there." Some weeks of delay that unseaworthy Pinta caused; but at last, on September 6th, they were once more started. Now, *to the west!* And, with their homes and the known world behind them, into the west they sailed!

49. Hardly had the land disappeared when the sailors, dismayed at their own boldness, began to be frightened enough. The steersmen let the vessels drift around a bit. "Steer to the *west!*" sternly cried Columbus. There was grumbling in the crew, and the admiral showed his wit by commencing then and there two records of the distance traveled each day. The record for the faithless sailors' edification showed fewer miles than the reality, and the truth of the matter no one knew but himself, from that day until he brought them safe to the other side. The fifth day a fragment of a ship drifted by them—"a wreck!" cried the sailors, and grew gloomy over the bad omen. One night a "remarkable bolt of fire" fell into the sea, and the superstitious men were panic-stricken. How could they go on in the face of this message from

heaven? But go on they must. This remarkable admiral said calmly: "Steer to the west."

50. As the days went on "they began to meet large patches of weeds, very green." "We must be near to land," said the sailors. "Perhaps some island," said the admiral; "but the continent we shall find further ahead." Another strange thing happened. That little compass, their only sure guide to Cathay, began to behave as if it too had lost its head over this foolhardy undertaking. The neighbors at home had warned them that the devil managed the compass; and this needle, never known to point anywhere but north, now pointed west of north! Was the devil steering them for hell? Heaven's fiery bolt had warned them; they had not heeded, and now the devil was tampering with the compass. Poor sailors! They looked fiercely on Columbus, and wished themselves well out of this business. But the admiral faced the strange occurrence quietly, though his heart may well have beat fearfully, and proceeded to investigate its cause. He soon announced it. "It is the north star that moves," he coolly informed the terrified men; "the needle is always true." The admiral was certainly a marvelously wise man, and the sailors said no more.

51. Eleven days out. No thickening of the sea yet, except with this mass of floating weed. No darkness, except the darkness of night. No nearer the sunset, and always at sunset-time that golden western path across the water. Weeds, weeds — vast stretches of weeds; they must betoken land; and a live crab discovered among them would surely seem to indicate it. The sea is smooth, the air clear. It is like "Andalusia in April, all but the nightingales," exclaims the admiral. What would you give to hear a nightingale just now, brave-hearted admiral, gazing into the moonlit infinity of silence that enspheres

you! You can not bear the crystal tension; go below to the relief of the narrow room and the journal faithfully kept!

52. More signs of land. They kill tunnies—sure sign, say the sailors. And all the signs are from the west, "where I hope the high God in whose hand is all victory will speedily direct us to land," writes the admiral. Even the faithless sailors begin to forget their sullen disapproval, and the three ships race merrily to see which shall first discover land. Great flocks of birds Alonzo Pinzon saw from the Pinta. "This very night we shall reach land, I believe!" he exulted; and the Pinta swiftly shot ahead, expecting to sight the shore at any moment. "There must be islands all about us," thought the admiral; "but we will not stay for them now. Straight to the west!"

53. Still no land, for all the signs and eager watching. Leagues of undulating weeds, but no land! And the faint-hearted sailors grumble again. They fear that they never shall "meet in these seas with a fair wind to return to Spain." A head-wind heartens them, but it quickly flits off laden with kisses for Andalusian sweethearts; and again the east wind fills the sails and carries them away, and away, and away!

54. Alonzo Pinzon and Columbus hold a conference, and Columbus, spreading out that dear map of the Atlantic lying between Europe and Asia, traces for the pilots the course they have pursued—a bold, straight westerly line—and shows them that they are now near the islands of the Asiatic coast. Inspired delusion! How did it happen that the distance you reckoned to Asia was just the distance that landed you on American shores!

55. Then, again, all eyes strain to the west, and the three little ships in that great circle of water steer swiftly on their unknown course to unknown lands. The excited

sailors can scarce do their work. "We are nearing land," the admiral says. He says it will be perhaps Cipango itself! "Think of the gold! and the dragons! Thou'rt a coward. In Cipango the king has his palace roofed and floored with gold—I remember the tale—and the pearls there are of a beautiful rose-color. If it is not Cipango, it will be still some other famous island, if not Cathay."

56. "But, bethink you of the monsters of those islands: we are like to meet two-headed men, they say, and lions, and beasts with men's heads!" "Ay, but the gold, the gold!" "What will gold be to thee, man, with a cannibal drinking thy blood? And there is somewhere there a valley of devils!" "Hist about that, there's no need to speak; any land were better than this dreary, endless ocean! Ay, ay, any land were better than this endless ocean!—I go to look for land. The admiral offers a reward to the man first discovering it. Ho! for the west, and the golden cities of Cathay!"

57. Monsters? devils? The admiral was a man of science and not of superstition, but those wild stories may well have made the night uncanny for him. Suddenly Alonzo Pinzon cried "Land!" and with praiseworthy prudence hastened to claim the reward. The admiral fell on his knees and thanked God. Alonzo Pinzon's crew sang the "Gloria"; the men of the Niña ran up the rigging, and shouted that the land was truly there. All night the excited men talked of nothing but that land, and the admiral changed their course to southwest, where it appeared to lie. Fast they sailed till morning, till noon, till afternoon, and then "discovered that what they had taken for land was nothing but clouds!" Oh, the fearful reaction after that tense twenty-four hours! "There is no further shore!" cried the sailors. "It is as they said: the sea goes on forever, and we are going to death!" The

admiral quietly ordered, "Sail on into the west." They could not gainsay him. He willed it, and they sailed on.

58. Weeds and birds still float and fly about the ships. "Fine weather and the sea smooth, many thanks to God," says the admiral. Alonzo Pinzon wished to seek the islands that might be near them. "No," said the admiral, "we shall not change our course." But the signs of land again brought reviving spirits and new hope to the men, and again the three ships try to outsail one another in the race for the first discovery. The Niña suddenly fired a salute—signal of land—but the land did not appear. Seeing flocks of birds flying southwest, Columbus altered his course to that direction, thinking that the birds knew better than he where land lay.

59. And three days more they sailed, watching eagerly the various signs—weeds, pelicans, passing birds—gazing, gazing, gazing upon that unbroken boundary line sweeping around the lonesome watery world! Only sky and sea, sea and sky, with lines of passing birds black across the one and the undulating weeds streaking the other—three little ships with spreading sails under the blue dome, that distant, limiting circle, delicately distinct, always curving in unbroken perfection. Ah! the calm cruelty of the smiling sea and sky!

60. "The admiral encouraged them in the best manner he could, representing the profits they were about to acquire, and adding that it was to no purpose to complain; having come so far, they had nothing to do but continue on to the Indies till, with the help of our Lord, they should arrive there." It is said, though Columbus does not record it, that now the sailors whispered about among themselves "that it would be their best plan to throw him quietly into the sea, and say he unfortunately fell in while he stood absorbed in looking at the stars!" If they did

plot such folly, they had sense enough not to carry it out.

61. So there was, indeed, nothing for it but to sail on. The next day brought more floating articles and newly excited expectancy. A cane, a log, a carved stick the Pinta found. Think of the way that carved stick passed from hand to hand! Carved with an iron tool, said one. Nay, I doubt it. See, they are waving a branch from the Niña's deck! Ho, the Pinta! "A stalk loaded with roseberries!" There *must* be land—or else the devil himself puts these signs in our way. Alonzo Pinzon, in the swift Pinta, kept ahead. Night came down. At ten the admiral, peering into the darkness, saw a light—was it one of those phantom lights reported to dance over these waters? A faint, glimmering light! "Pero Gutierrez, come here. I see a light! Look that way!"—"I see it too," said Pero. "Rodrigo Sanchez, come here—a light!" But Rodrigo Sanchez does not stand in the right place, and sees nothing at all. It was gone a moment. Then the admiral saw it moving up and down. "It *may* be an indication of land," admitted Rodrigo Sanchez; but Columbus was certain, and his orders were prompt and imperative: a strict watch to be kept upon the forecastle, and for him who should first see land a silken jacket and the reward promised by the king and queen.

62. At midnight the Pinta was still ahead. Ninety miles they had made since sunset. Look out for land, Alonzo Pinzon. Midnight—look sharp. No land. One o'clock—look sharp. No land. Two o'clock—what is it? Rodrigo de Triana has seen land, *land!* Make the signals, Alonzo Pinzon. Ho, the Santa Maria—*Land!* Ho, the Niña—*Land!* Take in the sails, wait now for the dawn—first dawn for Europe in the new world.

63. In the morning—it was Friday, October 12th,

five weeks since they saw the last of the Canaries—they found that the land was a small island with naked people on its shore. Here we are at last! We have accomplished it! Think of the exultation! Land with fitting ceremony, and take possession for the king and queen of Spain. Drop the small boat from the Santa Maria (put in your guns, lest the natives prove cannibals). Get in you, and you, and you, of the sailors; get in, Rodrigo de Escovedo, our secretary; you, of course, Rodrigo Sanchez, since the king sent you on purpose to bear witness to this occasion. Alonzo Pinzon and Vincent, carry your standards of the green cross; and the admiral bears the royal standard of our sovereigns. All aboard—put off the boat—row for the shore.

64. The curious natives flock about these strange beings, who come in winged ships, and have bodies covered with something besides skin—handsome natives, evidently no cannibals, and very obliging. No lions, or hippogriffs, or unicorns. But gold—yes, little pieces of it hanging about the savages' necks. They make signs that it comes from a land to the south. Cipango, thought Columbus, and set sail to find it. They were in the group of islands between North and South America, which we call the Bahamas and the West Indies. The first island discovered the natives called Guanahani, but Columbus named it San Salvador—"Holy Saviour."

65. They sailed about among them, hunting for gold and Cipango; bartering with the astonished natives; observing the land. Not quite equal to Mandeville's tales were the sights they saw, yet the luxuriant, tropical vegetation of the islands, the trees with luscious fruit and sweet perfume, the brilliant birds flitting through the green foliage, the marvelous fish flashing in the waters, the lizards darting across the paths, were wonderful

enough in their new beauty to the sea-weary eyes of the Europeans. "I saw no cannibals," says Columbus; but he heard of an island full of them. He heard, too, of the island of the Amazons, fierce, wild women, who use bows and spears, and are less like women than men. And there was an island where the inhabitants had no hair, and one where the people had tails. Mermaids he saw, but, adds the honest admiral, they were "not so like ladies as they are painted."

66. "Where do you get your gold?" says the admiral by signs to the islanders. "Cubanacan," say the natives. *Kubla Khan* flashes across the admiral's mind, and he sails off in renewed certainty. The island which the natives called Colba, or Cuba, he took for Cipango, and after much searching he came to it at last. When he did reach it, its size deceived him into thinking he had reached the continent, and messengers were straightway dispatched to seek the Grand Khan, with his marble bridges and golden towers. Columbus had brought along a letter to him from Ferdinand and Isabella, in which they tell him that, having heard of his love for them, and his wish to hear news from Spain, they now send their admiral to tell him of their health and prosperity! But the messengers could not find the khan. How could you know, Cristoforo Colombo, that you were only half way around the great world, and thousands of miles yet from Cathay!

THE REWARD.

67. America was discovered. The daring admiral never knew it. To the day of his death he thought the world was only half as large as it is, and that he had sailed west to Cathay.

68. America was discovered. Shout, Palos! Seven

months only have passed, and here come the heroes back again—back from Cipango and Cathay. Weep for joy, daughters and sweethearts and wives! Little children, gaze with fear upon those dark-skinned painted savages, and be consoled that they brought no dragons. Barcelona, ring your bells! The hero, Columbus, is coming in state! Crowd the streets, the doors, the windows, the roofs; king and queen receive him in magnificence. Hail to the man who has *succeeded!*

69. Three times afterward Columbus crossed the ocean to the new-found Indies, touching once the mainland of South America. No need to go into the details of his after life. How can one have the heart to tell of the quick subsiding of his triumph, the malicious envy of courtiers, the unreasonable discontent of subordinates, the selfish ambition of rivals, the wanton wickedness of the West Indian settlers; of his removal from the governorship, and his voyage home in chains, over *his* Atlantic; of his weakening health, his accumulating anxieties, his troubled old age? The peaceful death that closed it all in 1506 was relief to the bold spirit which injustice and pain could not subdue, but only hamper and fret. From the island of Jamaica, three years before his death, America's discoverer writes to his king and queen:

70. "For seven years was I at your royal court, where every one to whom the enterprise was mentioned treated it as ridiculous; but now there is not a man, down to the very tailors, who does not beg to be allowed to become a discoverer. . . . The lands in this part of the world which are now under your highnesses' sway are richer and more extensive than those of any other Christian power; and yet, after that I had, by the Divine will, placed them under your high and royal sovereignty, and

was on the point of bringing your majesties into the receipt of a very great and unexpected revenue, . . . I was arrested and thrown, with my two brothers, loaded with irons, into a ship, stripped and very ill treated, without being allowed any appeal to justice. . . . I was twenty-eight years old when I came into your highnesses' service, and now I have not a hair upon me that is not gray; my body is infirm, and all that was left to me, as well as to my brothers, has been taken away and sold, even to the frock that I wore, to my great dishonor. . . . I implore your highnesses to forgive my complaints. I am, indeed, in as ruined a condition as I have related; hitherto I have wept over others—may Heaven now have mercy upon me, and may the earth weep for me. With regard to temporal things, I have not even a blanca for an offering, and in spiritual things, I have ceased here in the Indies from observing the prescribed forms of religion. Solitary in my trouble, sick, and in daily expectation of death, surrounded by millions of hostile savages full of cruelty, and thus separated from the blessed sacraments of our holy church, how will my soul be forgotten if it be separated from the body in this foreign land! Weep for me, whoever has charity, truth, and justice!"

Ellen Coit Brown.

CHAPTER VI.

DEFENSE OF FREEDOM ON DUTCH DIKES.

1. AFTER the destruction of the Roman Empire all Europe was in a state of anarchy. The long domination of Rome, and the general acceptance of the Roman idea that "the state is everything and the individual man nothing," had unfitted the people for self-government. While Rome fell, the system of Rome, leading to absolute monarchy, persisted, and out of it grew the present governments of Europe. The conquering Goths brought in a modifying condition which changed the whole relations of monarch to people. In their social and political relations chieftains of tribes or clans divided power with the monarch, and for many centuries there was continuous warfare between these antagonistic ideas. This period is known as the "dark ages," for while it lasted there was little visible progress, and an apparent almost entire forgetfulness of the ancient civilizations.

2. During the dark ages roving bands of freebooters wandered about from place to place, engaged in robbery, rapine, and murder. To resist this systematic plunder the people placed themselves under the guardianship of some powerful chieftain in the vicinity, and paid a certain amount of their earnings for the privilege of enjoying the remainder. Hence there grew up, in the Gothic communities of Europe, that peculiar state of society known

as "the feudal system." A great chieftain or lord lived in a strong castle built for defense against neighboring lords. A retinue of soldiers was in immediate attendance, who, when not engaged in war, passed their time in hunting and debauchery. All the expenses and waste of the castle and its occupants were defrayed by the peasants who cultivated the lands, and who were all obliged to take up arms whenever their lord's dominions were invaded.

3. In process of time the taxes upon the people became so burdensome that they were reduced to the condition of serfs, when all their earnings, except enough to supply the barest necessaries of life, were taken from them in the shape of taxes and rents. A constantly increasing number were yearly taken from the ranks of the industrious to swell the numbers of the soldiery, until Europe seemed one vast camp.

4. The feudal system demanded little in the way of industry except agriculture and rude home manufactures to furnish food and clothing. Arms were purchased from other lands, the best being obtained from the higher civilization of the Moslems; but, as population increased, people began to congregate in centers and towns, and cities sprung up. These called for more varied industries, and a class of people soon became numerous who had little or no dependence upon the feudal lord. To protect themselves, craftsmen engaged in the same kind of work united and formed guilds, and the various guilds, though often warring with each other, united for the common defense. The leaders of the guilds gradually became the heads of notable burgher families who became influential and wealthy. As the cities became powerful the feudal system declined, and in many regions the powerful burghers were able to maintain their independence, not only against their old

lords, but also against the monarch who ruled many lordships.

5. Between the monarch and the lords there was a natural antagonism—the monarch endeavoring to gain power, and the lords endeavoring to retain their privileges. The burghers made use of these contending forces, and by sometimes siding with the one and sometimes with the other, they not only secured their own freedom, but laid the foundation for the freedom of the people which is now generally recognized, and which forms the very corner-stone of our republican institutions.

6. But the rise of the burgher class, and the evolution of human liberty through their work, was by no means an easy task. As the military spirit was dominant, the calling of an artisan was considered derogatory, and lords and soldiers looked down upon the industrious classes as inferior beings. Scott well represents this spirit in the speech of Rob Roy, the Highland chief, in his reply to the offer of Bailie Jarvie to get his sons employment in a factory: "Make my sons weavers! I would see every loom in Glasgow, beam, treadle, and shuttles, burnt in hell-fire sooner!" To break the force of the strong military power, and to secure to the industrious classes the rights of human beings, required a continuous warfare which lasted through many centuries, and which is far from being finished at the present time. But, thanks to the sturdy valor of the burghers of the middle ages, human liberty was maintained and transmitted to succeeding generations.

7 Hitherto in the history of the world mountains had been found necessary for the preservation of human liberty. Thermopylæ, Morgarten, Bannockburn, were all fought where precipitous hill-sides and narrow valleys prevented the champions of freedom from being over-

Dutch Dikes.

whelmed by numbers, and where a single man in defense of his home could wield more power than ten men in attack. The tyrants who lorded it over plains had learned by dear experience to shun mountains and avoid collisions with mountaineers; and, in case of controversies, they always endeavored to gain by stratagem what they could not obtain by force. Austrian tyranny had dashed itself in vain against the Alps, and English tyranny had turned back southward, thwarted and impotent, from the Scotch Highlands.

8. But it was to be demonstrated that liberty might have a home in other than mountain fastnesses. Along the North Sea is a stretch of country redeemed from the ocean. Great dikes, faced with granite from Norway, withstand the tempest from the turbulent ocean, and smaller dikes prevent inundations from rivers. In thousands of square miles the only land above sea-level is the summit of the dikes. In the polders or hollow places below the sea, and saved from destruction only by the dikes, is some of the richest and most productive land in Europe. Here prospered a teeming and industrious population. Agriculture, the parent of national prosperity, flourished as nowhere else. Manufactures and trade had followed in its train, until the hollow lands had become the beehive of Europe. The direction of the most vast commercial enterprises had been transferred from the lagoons of Venice to the cities of the dikes.

9. This country for centuries had constituted a part of the German Empire. At one side of the great lines of communication, and moored so far out to sea, it had been overlooked and neglected to a certain degree by the reigning dynasties; and out of this neglect grew its prosperity. While the rule of the central government was nearly nominal, the feudal lords never obtained a strong foothold in

the country, and the order and peace of the communities were preserved by municipal officers chosen by suffrage. In process of time wealthy burgher families fairly divided political influence with princes, and dictated a policy at once wise and humane. Extortioners were suppressed, industries fostered, and peace maintained.

10. In the religious controversies which followed the preaching of Luther, the eastern provinces of the hollow land almost exclusively espoused the new religion, while the western provinces clung as tenaciously to the old. While this difference in religious opinions gave rise to disputes, and tended toward the disruption of social relations, for many years toleration was practiced and peace preserved.

11. During the reign of Charles V as emperor of Germany, the lowland countries were permitted to go on in their career of prosperity, with the exception of a religious persecution. Charles was a bigot, and, for a time, he tried to put down heresy with a strong hand; but, finding the new doctrines firmly established in the hearts of the people, he relaxed his persecutions, and permitted things to take pretty much their own course.

12. On the abdication of Charles V, in 1555, Spain and the Leon countries fell to the lot of Philip II. Notwithstanding the riches which had poured into Spain from the plunder of Mexico and Peru, the Netherlands were the richest part of Philip's dominions, yielding him a princely revenue. But the free spirit manifested by these artisans, in their homes by the sea, was contrary to all Philip's ideas of government, and was constantly galling to his personal pride. So he determined to reduce his Teutonic subjects to the same degree of abject submission that he had the residents of the sunny lands of Spain. To give intensity to his resolve, Philip was a cold-blooded

bigot, and in carrying out his state designs he was also gratifying his religious animosities, and giving expression to his almost insane religious hatreds. His policy was directly calculated to ruin the most prosperous part of his own dominions—to "kill the goose which laid the golden egg."

13. Philip spent the first five years of his reign in the Netherlands, waiting the issue of a war in which he was engaged with France. During this period his Flemish and Dutch subjects began to have some experience of his government. They observed with alarm that the king hated the country and distrusted the people. He would speak no other language than Spanish; his counselors were Spaniards; he kept Spaniards alone about his person, and it was to Spaniards that all vacant posts were assigned. Besides, certain of his measures gave great dissatisfaction. He re-enacted the persecuting edicts against the Protestants which his father, in the end of his reign, had suffered to fall into disuse; and the severities which ensued began to drive hundreds of the most useful citizens out of the country, as well as to injure trade by deterring Protestant merchants from the Dutch and Flemish ports. Dark hints, too, were thrown out that he intended to establish an ecclesiastical court in the Netherlands similar to the Spanish Inquisition, and the spirit of Catholics as well as Protestants revolted from the thought that this chamber of horrors should ever become one of the institutions of their free land.

14. He had also increased the number of bishops in the Netherlands from five to seventeen; and this was regarded as the mere appointment of twelve persons devoted to the Spanish interest, who would help, if necessary, to overawe the people. Lastly, he kept the provinces full of Spanish troops, and this was in direct violation of a fundamental law of the country.

15. Against these measures the nobles and citizens complained bitterly, and from them drew sad anticipations of the future. Nor were they more satisfied with the address in which, through the bishop of Arras as his spokesman, he took farewell of them at a convention of the states held at Ghent previous to his departure to Spain. The oration recommended severity against heresy, and only promised the withdrawal of the foreign troops. The reply of the states was firm and bold, and the recollection of it must have rankled afterward in the revengeful mind of Philip. "I would rather be no king at all," he said to one of his ministers at the time, "than have heretics for my subjects." But suppressing his resentment in the mean time, he set sail for Spain in August, 1559, leaving his half-sister to act as his viceroy in the Netherlands.

16. At this juncture, while the Dutch were threatened by a complete subjugation of their liberties, a champion arose who in the end proved more than a match for Philip both in diplomatic fields and in military operations. This was William, Prince of Orange, one of the highest nobility, but with his whole heart in sympathy with the people. Inheriting a personality almost perfect in physical, mental, and moral vigor and harmony, he early manifested a prudence and wisdom which gained for him the entire confidence of the suspicious and experienced Charles V.

17. It was on the arm of William of Orange that Charles had leaned for support on that memorable day when, in the assembly of the states at Brussels, he rose feebly from his seat, and declared his abdication of the sovereign power; and it was said that one of Charles's last advices to his son Philip was to cultivate the goodwill of the people of the Netherlands, and especially to

defer to the counsels of the Prince of Orange. When, therefore, in the year 1555, Philip began his rule in the Netherlands, there were few persons who were either better entitled or more truly disposed to act the part of faithful and loyal advisers than William of Nassau, then twenty-two years of age.

18. But, close as had been William's relations to the late emperor, there were stronger principles and feelings in his mind than gratitude to the son of the monarch whom he had loved. He had thought deeply on the question, how a nation should be governed, and had come to entertain opinions very hostile to arbitrary power; he had observed what appeared to him, as a Catholic, gross blunders in the mode of treating religious differences; he had imbibed deeply the Dutch spirit of independence; and it was the most earnest wish of his heart to see the Netherlands prosperous and happy. Nor was he at all a visionary, or a man whose activity would be officious and troublesome; he was eminently a practical man, one who had a strong sense of what is expedient in existing circumstances; and his manner was so grave and quiet that he obtained the name of "William the Silent." Still, many things occurred during Philip's four years' residence in the Netherlands to make him speak out and remonstrate. He was one of those who tried to get the king to use gentler and more popular measures, and the consequence was that a decided aversion grew up in the dark and haughty mind of Philip to the Prince of Orange.

19. After the departure of Philip the administration of the Duchess of Parma produced violent discontent. The persecutions of the Protestants were becoming so fierce that, over and above the suffering inflicted on individuals, the commerce of the country was sensibly falling off. The establishment of a court like the Inqui-

sition was still in contemplation; Spaniards were still appointed to places of trust in preference to Flemings; and finally, the Spanish soldiers, who ought to have been removed long ago, were still burdening the country with their presence. The woes of the people were becoming intolerable; occasionally there were slight outbreaks of violence; and a low murmur of vehement feeling ran through the whole population, foreboding a general eruption. "Our poor fatherland!" they said to each other; "God has afflicted us with two enemies, water and Spaniards; we have built dikes and overcome the one, but how shall we get rid of the other? Why, if nothing better occurs, we know one way at least, and we shall keep it in reserve—we can set the two enemies against each other. We can break down the dikes, inundate the country, and let the water and the Spaniards fight it out between them."

20. About this time, too, the decrees of the famous Council of Trent, which had been convened in 1545 to take into consideration the state of the Church and the means of checking the new religion, and which had closed its sittings in the end of 1563, were made public; and Philip, the most zealous Catholic of his time, issued immediate orders for their being enforced both in Spain and in the Netherlands. In Spain the decrees were received as a matter of course, the council having authority over the Catholic people; but the attempt to force the mandates of an ecclesiastical body upon a people who neither acknowledged its authority nor believed in its truth, was justly regarded as an outrage, and the whole country burst out in a storm of indignation. In many places the decrees were not executed at all; and wherever the authorities did attempt to execute them, the people rose and compelled them to desist.

21. A political club or confederacy was organized among the nobility for the express purpose of resisting the establishment of the Inquisition. They bound themselves by a solemn oath "to oppose the introduction of the Inquisition, whether it were attempted openly or secretly, or by whatever name it should be called," and also to protect and defend each other from all the consequences which might result from their having formed this league.

22. Perplexed and alarmed, the regent implored the Prince of Orange and his two associates, Counts Egmont and Horn, to return to the council and give her their advice. They did so; and a speech of the Prince of Orange, in which he asserted strongly the utter folly of attempting to suppress opinion by force, and argued that "such is the nature of heresy that if it rests it rusts, but whoever rubs it whets it," had the effect of inclining the regent to mitigate the ferocity of her former edicts. Meanwhile the confederates were becoming bolder and more numerous. Assembling in great numbers at Brussels, they walked in procession through the streets to the palace of the regent, where they were admitted to an interview. In reply to their petition, she said she was willing to send one or more persons to Spain to lay the complaint before the king.

23. While the nobles and influential persons were thus preparing to co-operate, in case of a collision with the Spanish government, a sudden and disastrous movement occurred among the lower classes. It was stated and believed that the regent had given permission for the exercise of the Protestant form of worship, and throughout Flanders multitudes poured into the fields after the preachers. The reaction after the suppression of the previous years was very great, and the pent-up emotions

were easily kindled into rage against the Catholics. Led on by fanatics, the ignorant masses made a concerted attack upon the Catholic churches, shattering their windows, tearing up their pavements, and destroying all the objects of art which they contained. The cathedral at Antwerp was the special object of attack, and it was reduced to an almost hopeless ruin. The patriot nobles exerted their influence, and at last succeeded in suppressing the violence and in restoring order.

24. Before the news of this outburst had reached Spain, Philip had resolved to crush the confederacy and break the proud spirit of the Netherlands. Secret orders were given for the collection of troops; the regent was instructed to amuse the patriots until the means of punishing them were ready; and in a short time it was hoped that there would no longer be a patriot or a heretic in the Low Countries. It is easy to conceive with what rage and bitterness of heart Philip, while indulging these dreams, must have received intelligence of the terrible doings of the iconoclasts. But, as cautious and dissimulating as he was obstinate and revengeful, he concealed his intentions in the mean time, announced them to the regent only in secret letters and dispatches, and held out hopes in public to the patriots and people of the Netherlands that he was soon to pay them a visit in person to inquire into the condition of affairs.

25. William had secret intelligence of the purpose of Philip in time to avert its worst consequences. The man whom Philip sent into the Netherlands at the head of the army, as a fit instrument of his purpose of vengeance, was the Duke of Alva, a personage who united the most consummate military skill with the disposition of a ruffian, ready to undertake any enterprise however base. Such was the man who, at the age of sixty, in the month

of August, 1567, made his entry into the Netherlands at the head of an army of fifteen thousand men. One of his first acts was the arrest of the Counts Egmont and Horn. The regent resigned, and Alva was left in supreme control. Now ensued the grand struggle in the Netherlands. On the one hand was a nation of quiet, orderly people, industrious in a high degree, prosperous in their commerce, and disposed to remain peaceful subjects to a foreign monarch; on the other hand was a sovereign who, unthankful for the blessing of reigning over such a happy and well-disposed nation, and stimulated by passion and bigotry, resolved on compelling all to submit to his will on penalty of death.

26. Alva at once commenced his persecutions. Supported by his army, blood was shed like water. The Inquisition was established, and began its work of unspeakable horrors in the Netherlands. Patriots and Protestants in crowds left the country. The leading men of the Netherlands were arrested and executed. Under circumstances of extreme ferocity Counts Egmont and Horn were beheaded at Brussels. Overwhelming taxes were imposed upon the people, and during the short period of his administration Alva executed eighteen thousand patriots, including many Catholics; for, in his rage against the free spirit of the Netherlanders, he recognized no distinction in condition or in religious belief.

27. In the mean time the Prince of Orange was active in devising means to liberate his unfortunate country from the terrible scourge to which it was subjected. For five years he battled incessantly against the Spanish power. Now he entered into combination with the English and now with the French, with the vain hope of obtaining a sufficient force to drive the Spaniards out of the country. Twice he raised an army and marched to the aid of the

brave burghers, who still maintained their independence, and both times was defeated by the superior force and generalship of Alva. He organized a fleet which ravaged the coast, captured vessels laden with provisions for Alva's army, and defended the ports within reach of their guns. When the shattered remains of William's last army retreated across the German frontier, it seemed that the people of the Netherlands were about to be left to their fate.

28. But sixty cities and towns were now in revolt, and, unless they were recovered, Philip could no longer be considered the king of the Netherlands. Nothing was left but the slow process of siege operations. Haarlem held out seven months, and cost the Spaniards ten thousand men. It surrendered at last under the promise of an amnesty to its defenders, when they were murdered by thousands in cold blood. But Philip was dissatisfied with Alva for his slow progress, and for his execution of Catholics as well as Protestants; and in 1753, after five years' rule, he recalled him, and, with characteristic ingratitude, neglected and ill-treated him for his faithful but bloody services.

29. Don Luis Requesens succeeded the Duke of Alva as governor of the Netherlands and as commander of the Spanish army. While a zealous Catholic, he seems to have been a much more humane and just man than Alva. He began his administration by abolishing the most obnoxious measures of his predecessor, thus changing the whole tone of the government. Had he been left to follow his own counsels in everything, he doubtless would have come to an understanding with the Prince of Orange, and established peace upon a permanent basis. But the king was obstinately determined to capture the revolted cities and punish his rebel subjects, and the general was

obliged to continue the war. At this time William was besieging Middleburg, on the island of Zealand, and one of the first acts of the newly-appointed governor was to raise the siege. To this end he caused a large fleet to be assembled, and under the command of two experienced admirals he sent it down the Scheldt to the relief of Middleburg. The Prince of Orange immediately hastened to the critical spot, and gave direction to patriot operations. The Holland ships were collected, and a great naval battle took place on January 29, 1574. Although their force was much the greater, the Spaniards had little chance upon the water in a contest with the half-amphibious inhabitants of the Low Countries. The smaller vessels of the Prince of Orange fell upon the Spanish fleet with a ferocity which they could not withstand, and the result was a complete victory, with the destruction of their principal vessels. Middleburg soon after surrendered to the patriots, and the sway of William over the maritime provinces was rendered complete.

30. In April an army from Germany, raised through the influence of the Prince of Orange, and commanded by his brother, Count Henry of Nassau, marched into the Low Countries; but the Spaniards dominated the land as the Dutch the sea, and the relief army was defeated and Count Henry was killed. This defeat, however, to the patriot cause, was almost equal to a victory. The Spanish troops, who had long been without pay, became mutinous and unmanageable, and before they could be appeased much precious time was lost. The Prince of Orange made the best use of this time. The revolted cities were strengthened and supplied with provisions, and every preparation made for both defensive and offensive war. But, best of all, the Dutch admiral boldly sailed up the Scheldt, captured forty of the Spanish vessels, and sunk many more.

31. At length the Spanish general was once more ready to continue his aggressive movements, and he proceeded to lay siege to the populous city of Leyden. The story of this siege is one of the most spirit-stirring in the annals of heroism. Leyden stands in a low situation, in the midst of a labyrinth of rivulets and canals. That branch of the Rhine which still retains the name of its upper course passes through the middle of it, and from this stream such an infinity of canals are derived that it is difficult to say whether the water or the land possesses the greater space. By these canals the ground on which the city stands is divided into a great number of small islands, united together by bridges.

32. For five months all other operations were suspended; all the energy of Requesens, on the one hand, was directed toward getting possession of the city, and all the energy of the Prince of Orange, on the other hand, toward assisting the citizens, and preventing it from being taken. The issue depended entirely, however, on the bravery and resolution of the citizens of Leyden themselves. Pent up within their walls, they had to resist the attacks and stratagems of the besiegers; and all that the Prince of Orange could do was to occupy the surrounding country, harass the besiegers as much as possible, and enable the citizens to hold out, by conveying to them supplies of provisions and men.

33. There was not in the city a single scion of a noble family. There were no men trained to military operations. It was a city of artisans and tradesmen, and the Spaniards expected scarcely more than a show of resistance from a foe so ignoble. As well might the sheep resist a pack of ravening wolves as the men of the counting-house and workshop resist the best trained soldiers of Europe. But nobly, nay, up to the highest heroic pitch

of human nature, did the citizens behave! They had to endure a siege in its most dreary form—that of a blockade. Instead of attempting to storm the town, Valdez, the Spanish general, resolved to reduce it by the slow process of starvation. For this purpose he completely surrounded the town by a circle of forts more than sixty in number; and the inhabitants thus saw themselves walled completely in from the rest of the earth, with its growing crops and its well-filled granaries, and restricted entirely to whatever quantity of provisions there happened to be on the small spot of ground on which they walked up and down. Their only means of communication with the Prince of Orange was by carrier-pigeons trained for the purpose.

34. One attempt was made by them to break through the line of blockade, for the sake of keeping possession of a piece of pasture-ground for their cattle; but it was unsuccessful; and they began now to work day and night in repairing their fortifications, so as to resist the Spanish batteries when they should begin to play. Like fire pent up, the patriotism of the inhabitants burned more fiercely and brightly; every man became a hero, every woman an orator, and words of flashing genius were spoken and deeds of wild bravery done, such as would have been impossible except among twenty thousand human beings living in the same city, and all roused at once to the same unnatural pitch of emotion.

35. The two leading spirits were John van der Dors, the commander, better known by his Latinized name of Dousa; and Peter van der Werf, the burgomaster. Plebeian names these, but loftier natures never possessed the hearts of kings or nobles! Beside their deeds, the chivalry of knighthood looks trivial and mean. Under the management of these two men every precaution was adopted for

the defense of the city. The resolution come to was, that the last man among them should die of want rather than admit the Spaniards into the town. Coolly, and with a foresight thoroughly Dutch, Dousa and Van der Werf set about making an inventory of all that was eatable in the town: corn, cattle—nay, even horses and dogs; calculating how long the stock could last at the rate of so much a day to every man and woman in the city; adopting means to get the whole placed under the management of a dispensing committee; and deciding what should be the allowance per head at first, so as to prevent their stock from being eaten up too fast.

36. It was impossible, however, to collect all the food into one fund, or to regulate its consumption by municipal arrangements; and, after two months had elapsed, famine had commenced in earnest, and those devices for mitigating the gnawings of hunger began to be employed which none but starving men would think of. Not only the flesh of dogs and horses, but roots, weeds, nettles—everything green that the eye could detect shooting up from the earth—was ravenously eaten. Many died of want, and thousands fell ill. Still they held out, and indignantly rejected the offers made to them by the besiegers.

37. "When we have nothing else," said Dousa, in reply to a message from Valdez, "we will eat our left hands, keeping the right to fight with." Once, indeed, hunger seemed to overcome patriotism, and for some days crowds of gaunt and famished wretches moved along the streets, crying: "Let the Spaniards in; for God's sake let them in!" Assembling with hoarse clamor at the house of Van der Werf, they demanded that he should give them food or surrender. "I have no food to give you," was the burgomaster's reply, "and I have sworn that I will

not surrender to the Spaniards; but, if my body will be of any service to you, tear me in pieces, and let the hungriest of you eat me." The poor wretches went away, and thought no more of surrendering.

38. The thought of the Prince of Orange night and day was how to render assistance to the citizens of Leyden—how to convey provisions into the town. He had collected a large supply, but, with all his exertions, could not raise a sufficient force to break through the blockade. In this desperate extremity the Dutch resolved to have recourse to that expedient which they had kept in reserve until it should be clear that no other was left—they would break their dikes, open their sluices, inundate the whole level country around Leyden, and wash the Spaniards and their forts utterly away!

39. It was truly a desperate measure, and it was only in the last extremity that they could bring themselves to think of it. All that fertile land, which the labor of ages had drained and cultivated—to see it converted into a sheet of water! There could not possibly be a sight more unseemly and melancholy to a Dutchman's eyes. But, when the measure was once resolved upon, they set to work with a heartiness and zeal greater than that which had attended their building. Hatchets, hammers, spades, and pickaxes were in requisition; and by the labor of a single night the work of ages was demolished and undone. The water, availing itself of the new inlets, poured over the flat country, and in a short time the whole of the region between Leyden and Rotterdam was flooded.

40. The Spaniards, terror-stricken, at first resolved upon immediate flight; but, seeing that the water did not rise above a certain level, they recovered their courage, and, though obliged to abandon their forts, which were stationed upon the low grounds, they persevered in the

blockade. But there was another purpose to be served by the inundation of the country beside that of washing away the Spaniards, and the Prince of Orange made preparations for effecting it. He had caused two hundred flat-bottomed boats to be built, and loaded with provisions; these now began to row toward the famished city. The inhabitants saw them coming; they watched them eagerly advancing across the waters, fighting their way past the Spanish forts, and bringing bread to them. But it seemed as if Heaven itself had become cruel; for a north wind was blowing, and, so long as it continued to blow, the waters would not be deep enough for the boats to reach the city. They waited for days, every eye fixed on the vanes; but still the wind continued in the north, though never within the memory of the oldest citizen had it blown in that direction so long at that time of year. Many died in sight of the vessels that contained the food which would have kept them alive; and those who survived shuffled along the streets, living skeletons instead of men!

41. But the sea did not at last desert the brave men who had so long dominated it. At the last extremity it roused itself and swept down in its might upon the doomed Spaniards. When but two days stood between the starving citizens and death, lo! the vanes trembled and veered round; the wind shifted first to the northwest, blowing the sea-tides with hurricane force into the mouth of the rivers, and then to the south, driving the waters directly toward the city. The remaining forts of the Spaniards were quickly begirt with water. The Spaniards themselves, pursued by the Zealanders in their boats, were either drowned or shot swimming, or fished out with hooks fastened to the end of poles, and killed with the sword. Several bodies of them, however, effected their escape. The citizens had all crowded at the

gates to meet their deliverers. With bread in their hands they ran through the streets; and many who had outlived the famine died of surfeit. The same day they met in one of the churches—a lean and sickly congregation—with the magistrates at their head, to return thanks to Almighty God for his mercy.

42. The citizens of Leyden had performed their duty nobly and well. It was a triple service—they had driven away from their city the hated Spaniard; they had secured the freedom of their country; and they had preserved liberty for mankind. No nobler deeds are chronicled in all history than this long battle with death, than this silent, uncomplaining endurance during the long weeks, while the life-giving succors were delayed by adverse winds. As a recompense to the people of Leyden for their heroic conduct, the Prince of Orange gave them the choice of exemption from taxes for a certain number of years, or of having a university established in the city; and, much to their honor, they preferred the latter. The University of Leyden was accordingly established in 1575. At one time it attained so high a reputation for learning that Leyden was styled the Athens of the West.

CHAPTER VII.

THE INVINCIBLE ARMADA.

1. In 1588 the "Invincible Armada" sailed from Spain into the high seas. To understand the nature of this formidable naval armament and the reasons for its sailing, we must take a brief survey of the condition of Europe at this period of the world's history.

SPAIN BEFORE THE ARMADA.

2. At this time Spain was the most powerful of the monarchies of Europe. Many causes had conspired to give her this pre-eminence. About one hundred years before, the two principal provinces, Castile and Aragon, were united by the marriage of their sovereigns, Isabella and Ferdinand. In 1492 the Moors were subjugated, uniting the whole peninsula under one government. In the same year, under the auspices of the Spanish sovereigns, Columbus discovered the New World, giving additional luster to the Spanish name and a new impulse to Spanish adventure.

3. Thirty years later, Mexico and Peru had been overrun and plundered by Cortes and Pizarro, and the treasures of millions of people, accumulated through many centuries, became a possession of the Spanish people; raising them to a degree of opulence unknown since the

time of the most illustrious of the Roman emperors. In consequence of this wealth, commerce expanded, large cities grew up along the courses of the navigable rivers, and all branches of industry were aroused to a state of great activity.

4. In 1516 Spain and Austria were united under the Emperor Charles V, grandson of Ferdinand and Isabella; and, during his reign, the united kingdoms arose to a height of power almost equal to that of the empire of Charlemagne. The dominion of Charles extended from the Atlantic to the steppes of Poland, and from the Mediterranean to the Baltic. It included all of Western Continental Europe, except France and Southern Italy. In 1556 Charles abdicated his throne, and divided his empire, giving Austria and Germany to his brother Ferdinand, and Spain and the Low Countries of Holland and Belgium to his son Philip II.

5. Spain was now rich and powerful. Her armies were large, and were commanded by the most experienced military officers of Europe. Material progress showed itself on every side. The richest commerce of the world poured its wealth into her ports. A new intellectual life was aroused, which found expression in literature and schools. All the conditions seemed to indicate that the Spanish people were about to lead Europe in the direction of a higher civilization.

CHARACTER AND POLICY OF PHILIP II

6. But soon all this changed. Philip was vain, bigoted, and ambitious. In his administration of public affairs he seemed to have but two objects in view, to augment Spanish power, and to cause his own religious creed to be universally accepted. To promote these objects he had

no scruples in regard to means. His own people were tortured and executed by the thousand. By this savage policy he stamped out heresy, placed freedom of thought under a ban, and put an end to the intellectual progress of the country. In his dealings with other nations his diplomacy included all the arts of chicanery and deceit.

7. Two formidable obstacles stood in the way of the realization of his plans. Heretical England had become a strong naval power, and English ships captured his treasure-vessels laden with the spoils of the countries he had plundered. The eagles of the sea despoiled the wolves of the main of their ill-got gains. The second trouble was nearer home. The people of the Low Countries revolted alike from his government and his creed. To remove these obstacles was the first step toward the attainment of his larger ambitions.

8. In regard to England, Philip ventured upon a master-stroke of policy. He sought the hand of Mary, the newly crowned Queen of England, and married her. By this step he hoped and expected to extinguish dissent in England as he had done in his own dominions, to gradually usurp the government, and to make English naval supremacy subserve the interests of Spain.

9. But Philip was sorely disappointed. Mary, though narrow and bigoted, and at one with him in creed, had still English blood in her; and English independence had been sturdily maintained through too many centuries to be surrendered to any power or on any pretext. The English Parliament also interfered and refused to crown him jointly with Mary. So Philip found himself united to a sickly, peevish wife of twice his age, and entirely powerless to effect the purposes he had in view.

10. Three or four years passed in fruitless intrigue. Punishments for heresy were frequent, but the fires of

persecution never blazed so fiercely in the cooler atmosphere of England as in Spain, and the victims of the stake could be counted singly instead of by the thousand. Then Mary died, and Elizabeth ascended the throne of England. The new queen declined the honor of Philip's hand which was tendered her, and she zealously espoused the cause of the English church. The hunted turned hunters, and the last fires of English persecution were lit by those whom the stake had threatened all through the dreary years of Mary's reign. This change of front and the gradual amelioration of penalties which followed show that persecutions are not the monopoly of any sect, but are rather the manifestations of an irresponsible power in a semi-barbarous age.

11. Philip retired angry and disgusted. The contemptuous refusal of his hand by Elizabeth was a terrible shock to his personal pride; the triumph of the new church inflamed his bigotry; and the sturdy independence of the English people was a severe blow to his pride of country. He brooded over the situation and determined to resent the slights—personal and public—which had been put upon him.

12. From his purpose he was for a time diverted by the attitude of his rebellious subjects in Belgium. Maddened to ferocity by the failure of his plans, he devoted the whole people to destruction, and he sent his best-equipped armies, under the terrible Duke of Alva, to devastate the cities of the dikes as Pizarro had destroyed the homes of the Incas. After innumerable atrocities, and the wholesale slaughter of men, women, and children, the remnant of freedom was preserved by the obstinacy of the Dutch burghers, the wise policy of William the Silent, the aid of the sea, and the succor furnished by Elizabeth.

The Spanish Armada.

13. Here, again, was practical defeat. His cherished purposes were thwarted, and the high hope of his life was gone. Nothing was left but despair and revenge. At this time Philip began to exhibit in a marked degree the madness which overshadowed the last years of his life. His hatred of England grew from day to day, and at last took shape in a determination to make one supreme effort to conquer his rival, and to check the rising free thought of the English people. For years the preparations went on for the great conflict, and in 1588, twenty years after the accession of Elizabeth to the throne, everything was ready.

ENGLAND'S POWER TO RESIST THE ARMADA.

14. And what of England and of her ability to resist this formidable attack? For a hundred years before the beginning of the sixteenth century, the civil wars of the Roses had desolated the country and put an end to national growth. For the next fifty years, and until the commencement of the reign of Elizabeth, violence and bloodshed were so common that the population barely maintained its own. In 1588 the whole number of people in England and Wales was estimated at four millions, about one third of the population of Spain.

15. But England possessed two elements of strength—her people, although differing in creed and often warring with one another, were intensely patriotic, and were united as one man against a foreign foe; and the ships of England, manned by English crews and commanded by her great captains—the legitimate successors of the old Vikings—dominated the seas. No enterprise was too hazardous for these hardy mariners to undertake, and no disparity of force ever induced them to pause. Philip

was often wrought to frenzy as he saw these bold corsairs capture his treasure-ships and ravage his coasts in sight of his invincible but impotent armies.

16. The mode of attack which Philip determined upon consisted of two distinct but co-operative movements. A formidable army of invasion, under the Duke of Parma, the most experienced and skillful commander in Europe, was stationed at the several ports of the Low Countries, opposite the British coast, from Dunkirk east. Innumerable transports were provided to convey this host across the Channel, and, once on English ground, an easy and triumphant march to London was expected. The second part of the grand expedition consisted of an immense fleet of the largest vessels ever built, under the command of the Duke of Medina Sidonia, which was to drive away the English ships and convoy the army of Parma to the English shore. This fleet was christened by the Spaniards "The Invincible Armada."

17. "Philip hastened his preparations with all the energy he could command. In every port resounded the axe and hammer of the ship-builder; in every arsenal blazed the flames of busy forges. All Spanish Europe echoed with the din of arms. Provisions were amassed in a thousand granaries; soldiers were daily mustered on the parade-grounds, drilled, and accustomed to the use of arquebus and cannon. Carts and wagons were built in hundreds for the conveyance of stores; spades, mattocks, and baskets were got ready for the pioneers; iron and brass ordnance were cast, and leaden shot melted in enormous quantities; nor were the instruments of torture—the thumb-screw and the 'jailer's daughter'—forgotten."

18. In 1587 the preparations were nearly completed, and the Armada was about ready to sail, when a knowledge of its destination became known to Sir Francis

Drake, the great English commander. Without considering the disparity of force, the old sea-king, with a fleet of swift-sailing vessels, made a sudden descent upon the port of Cadiz, where the ships of the Armada were at anchor. Many of the larger vessels escaped by taking refuge under the guns of the forts, but the city was lit up by the blaze of one hundred and fifty burning ships, and the great enterprise was delayed for another year.

SAILING OF THE ARMADA.

19. But this disaster only called forth greater exertions. The maimed vessels were repaired, new ones were built, and at length one hundred and thirty-two ships, many of them the largest ever known at the time, were ready to sail. They carried three thousand guns and thirty thousand men. On May 3d the Armada sailed from the mouth of the Tagus, but a great gale dispersed the ships, and obliged them to put back into port to repair. Surely God did not smile upon the beginning of a warfare carried on in his name! It was not until July 12th that the fleet finally sailed from Corunna on its mission of destruction, and to meet its fate.

20. To cope with this formidable force, the whole British navy could muster only thirty-six vessels, all much smaller than the largest of the Spanish ships. But, in consideration of the great danger, merchants and private gentlemen fitted out vessels at their own expense, and by midsummer a fleet of one hundred and ninety-seven ships was placed at the disposal of the British admiral. In tonnage, number of guns, and number of men, the strength of the whole fleet was about one half that of the Armada.

21. But all England was aroused. For more than five centuries this was the first foreign invasion that had threat-

ened her shores. The years of preparation had given time for the avowed purposes of Philip to become known throughout the kingdom. There was anxiety everywhere, for no one knew where and when the blow was to be struck; but there was no thought of submission, and all England stood alert, eagerly watching and waiting. Much to Philip's disappointment and chagrin, the great Catholic families of England rallied to their country's defense as readily as their Protestant neighbors, and all Englishmen stood shoulder to shoulder in this supreme moment of the nation's peril. Vessels patrolled the shores, to give notice of the coming ships; soldiers drilled in every hamlet; and on the hill-tops piles of fagots were placed so that signal-fires might speedily send the news to the remotest parts of the kingdom.

WAITING FOR THE ARMADA.

22. Canon Kingsley has given a graphic picture of England's great naval commanders, when the news was received that the Armada was off the coast. He supposes them assembled at Plymouth on the 19th of July, engaged in the then favorite game of bowls.

23. "Those soft, long eyes and pointed chin you recognize already. They are Sir Walter Raleigh's. The fair young man in the flame-colored suit at his side is Lord Sheffield; opposite them stand Lord Sheffield's uncle, Sir Richard Grenville, and the stately Lord Charles Howard of Effingham, Lord High Admiral of England; next to him is his son-in-law, Sir Robert Southwell, captain in her Majesty's service.

24. "But who is that short, sturdy, plainly dressed man, who stands with legs a little apart, and hands behind his back, looking up with keen gray eyes into the face of

each speaker? His cap is in his hand, so you can see the bullet-head of crisp brown hair and the wrinkled forehead as well as the high cheek-bones, the short square face, the broad temples, the thick lips, which are yet as firm as granite. A coarse, plebeian stump of a man; yet the whole figure and attitude are those of boundless determination, self-possession, energy; and, when at last he speaks a few blunt words, all eyes are turned respectfully on him, for his name is Francis Drake.

25. "A burly, grizzled elder, in greasy, sea-stained garments, contrasting oddly with the huge gold chain about his neck, waddles up, as if he had been born, and had lived ever since, in a gale of wind at sea. The upper half of his sharp, dogged visage seems of a brick-red leather, the brow of badger's fur, and, as he claps Drake on the back, with a broad Devon accent he shouts, 'Be you a-coming to drink your wine, Francis Drake, or be you not? saving your presence my lord.' The lord high admiral only laughs, and bids Drake go and drink his wine, for John Hawkins, admiral of the fleet, is the patriarch of Plymouth seamen, if Drake is the hero.

26. "So they push through the crowd, wherein is many another man whom we would gladly have spoken with face to face on earth. Martin Frobisher and John Davis are sitting on that bench, smoking tobacco from long silver pipes; and by them are Fenton and Wishington, who have both tried to follow Drake's path around the world, and failed, though by no fault of their own. The short, prim man, in the huge yellow ruff, is Richard Hawkins, the admiral's hereafter famous son.

27. "But hark! the boom of a single gun seaward directs the attention of every one to a small armed vessel staggering up the sound under a press of canvas. A boat puts off; its oars flash quickly in the sun; the cap-

tain lands, and, inquiring for the lord high admiral, is quickly brought into his presence. He has discovered the formidable array of the Spaniards bearing down with the wind like so many floating castles, the ocean seeming to groan under the weight of their heavy burdens. The lord high admiral proposes to hold counsel with his principal officers; but, says Drake, with a hearty laugh: 'Let us play out our play; there will be plenty of time to win the game and beat the Spaniards, too.'

28. "The game was played out steadily, and, the last cast having been thrown, Drake and his comrades leaped into their boats and rowed swiftly to their respective ships. With so much skill did Howard and his lieutenants direct the movements of their squadrons that, before morning, sixty of the best English ships had warped out of Plymouth Harbor."

HOW THE NEWS SPREAD THROUGH ENGLAND.

29. While preparations had been made to meet the Armada, there seems to have been a half expectation on the part of the government that something would occur to prevent its sailing. Until the very last, Elizabeth and her counselors appeared to place more confidence in diplomacy and political combinations than in the powers of Sir Francis Drake and his coadjutors. So, when the Armada was seen off the coast, the signal-fires were kindled, and the whole kingdom was soon ablaze. The stirring verse of Macaulay best describes the spread of the news, the alarm, the anxiety, and the grand uprising of the whole people:

30. Attend, all ye who list to hear
  Our noble England's praise;
I tell of the thrice-famous deeds
  She wrought in ancient days,

When that great fleet invincible
  Against her bore in vain
The richest spoils of Mexico,
  The stoutest hearts of Spain.

31. It was about the lovely close
  Of a warm summer day,
There came a gallant merchant-ship
  Full sail to Plymouth Bay;
Her crew hath seen Castile's black fleet,
  Beyond Aurigny's isle,
At earliest twilight, on the waves,
  Lie heaving many a mile.

32. At sunrise she escaped their van,
  By God's especial grace;
And the tall Pinta, till the noon,
  Had held her close in chase.

33. Forthwith a guard at every gun
  Was placed along the wall;
The beacon blazed upon the roof
  Of Edgecumbe's lofty hall;
Many a light fishing-bark put out
  To ply along the coast,
And with loose rein and bloody spur
  Rode inland many a post.

34. With his white hair unbonneted,
  The stout old sheriff comes;
Before him march the halberdiers;
  Behind him sound the drums;
His yeomen round the market cross
  Make clear an ample space;
For there behooves him to set up
  The standard of her Grace.

35. And haughtily the trumpets peal,
  And gayly dance the bells,
As slow upon the laboring wind
  The royal blazon swells.
Look how the Lion of the sea
  Lifts up his ancient crown,
And underneath his deadly paw
  Treads the gay lilies down.

36. So stalked he when he turned to flight,
  On that famed Picard field,*
Bohemia's plume, and Genoa's bow,
  And Cæsar's eagle shield.
So glared he when at Agincourt
  In wrath he turned to bay,
And crushed and torn beneath his claws
  The princely hunters lay.

37. Ho! Strike the flag-staff deep, Sir Knight:
  Ho! scatter flowers, fair maids:
Ho! gunners, fire a loud salute:
  Ho! gallants, draw your blades:
Thou sun, shine on her joyously;
  Ye breezes, waft her wide;
Our glorious SEMPER EADEM,
  The banner of our pride.

38. The freshening breeze of eve unfurled
  That banner's massy fold;
The parting gleam of sunshine kissed
  That haughty scroll of gold;
Night sank upon the dusky beach,
  And on the purple sea,
Such night in England ne'er hath been
  Nor e'er again shall be.

* The battle of Crécy, won by the Black Prince.

39. From Eddystone to Berwick bounds,
   From Lynn to Milford Bay,
That time of slumber was as bright
   And busy as the day;
For swift to east and swift to west
   The ghastly war-flame spread,
High on St. Michael's Mount it shone:
   It shone on Beachy Head.

40. Far on the deep the Spaniard saw,
   Along each southern shire,
Cape beyond cape, in endless range,
   Those twinkling points of fire.
The fisher left his skiff to rock
   On Tamar's glittering waves:
The rugged miners poured to war
   From Mendip's sunless caves:

41. O'er Longleat's towers, o'er Cranbourne's oaks,
   The fiery herald flew:
And roused the shepherds of Stonehenge,
   The rangers of Beaulieu.
Right sharp and quick the bells all night
   Rang out from Bristol town,
And e'er the day three hundred horse
   Had met on Clifton down;

42. The sentinel on Whitehall gate
   Looked forth into the night,
And saw o'erhanging Richmond Hill
   The streak of blood-red light.
Then bugle's note and cannon's roar
   The death-like silence broke,
And with one start, and with one cry,
   The royal city woke.

43. At once on all her stately gates
Arose the answering fires;
At once the wild alarum clashed
From all her reeling spires;
From all the batteries of the Tower
Pealed loud the voice of fear;
And all the thousand masts of Thames
Sent back a louder cheer:

44. And from the farthest wards was heard
The rush of hurrying feet,
And the broad streams of pikes and flags
Rushed down each roaring street;
And broader still became the blaze,
And louder still the din,
As fast from every village round
The horse came spurring in:

45. And eastward straight from wild Blackheath
The warlike errand went,
And roused in many an ancient hall
The gallant squires of Kent.
Southward from Surrey's pleasant hills
Flew those bright couriers forth;
High on bleak Hampstead's swarthy moor
They started for the north;

46. And on, and on, without a pause
Untired they bounded still;
All night from tower to tower they sprang;
They sprang from hill to hill:
Till the proud peak unfurled the flag
O'er Darwin's rocky dales,
Till like volcanoes flared to heaven
The stormy hills of Wales;

47. Till twelve fair counties saw the blaze
On Malvern's lonely height,
Till streamed in crimson on the wind
The Wrekin's crest of light,
Till broad and fierce the star came forth
On Ely's stately fane,
And tower and hamlet rose in arms
O'er all the boundless plain;

48. Till Belvoir's lordly terraces
The sign to Lincoln sent,
And Lincoln sped the message on
O'er the wide vale of Trent;
Till Skiddaw saw the fire that burned
On Gaunt's embattled pile,
And the red glare on Skiddaw roused
The burghers of Carlisle.

THE PRELIMINARY SKIRMISH.

49. It was on Saturday, July 20th, a dull, misty day, that the two great fleets, which represented the cause of freedom on the one side and the longing after universal empire on the other, came in sight of each other. The great Armada, with its huge galleons in battle array extending over a space of many miles, was suffered to sail up the Channel, past Plymouth Harbor, without molestation. This was in accordance with the general plan of attack which had been agreed upon.

50. The superior force of the Spaniards caused no fear, but rather a grim determination to overwhelm and destroy. The universal sentiment that seemed to prevail among all classes of Englishmen concerning their country finds fitting expression in the words which Shakespeare puts into the mouth of John of Gaunt:

"This royal throne of kings, this sceptered isle,
This earth of majesty, this seat of Mars,
This other Eden, demi-paradise;
This fortress, built by Nature for herself
Against infection and the hand of war;
This happy breed of men, this little world;
This precious stone set in the silver sea,
Which serves it in the office of a wall,
Or as a moat defensive to a house,
Against the envy of less happier lands;
This blessed spot, this earth, this realm, this England,
Dear for her reputation through the world."

51. To guard this favored spot, and to protect its soil from the polluting footstep of the hated Spaniard, mariners went forth to do or die. It was now, in the moment of supreme peril, that the courage, hardihood, and skill of England's great navigators gained in battle with the elements in the unknown seas of the North and West, and in many a strife against fearful odds with their Spanish foes, were found to be equal to the occasion and sufficient to insure the safety of their country.

52. On Sunday morning, July 21st, the English ships commenced their attacks upon their unwieldy antagonists. "The Spanish ships," says Motley, "seemed arrayed for a pageant in honor of a victory won. Arranged in the form of a crescent whose horns were seven miles asunder, those gilded towers and floating castles, with their brilliant standards and martial music, bore slowly up the Channel. The admiral, the 'Golden Duke,' stood in his private shot-proof tower, on the deck of his great galleon, the Saint Martin, surrounded by guards of infantry and captains of cavalry, no better acquainted than himself with naval tactics.

53. "And just as the gadfly hovers about and stings the horse, which is all unable to escape from its tiny ene-

my, so round the heavy galleons and unwieldy ships of Spain the light English vessels, commanded by able and experienced seamen, hovered with the utmost freedom. Their superior tactics soon obtained the advantage of the wind, enabling them at intervals to cannonade their enemies with great effect, while they themselves escaped out of range at pleasure, and easily avoided the tremendous discharge of the Spanish ordnance.

54. "In vain the Golden Duke attempted to bring on a general engagement. Howard and Drake were well aware that in a ship-to-ship fight the strongest would necessarily conquer, and that their only hope of success lay in keeping close upon the enemy's flanks, or following at his heels, cutting off a stray galleon, making a dash into his ill-managed squadrons, and so gradually but surely reducing his strength, until they could venture to give him battle on more equal terms."

55. "The Armada," Mr. Froude says, "made sail and attempted to close. To Medina Sidonia's extreme astonishment, it seemed at the pleasure of the English to leave him or allow him to approach them as they chose. The high-towered, broad-bowed galleons moved like Thames barges piled with hay, while the sharp, low English ships sailed at near two feet to the Spaniards' one and shot away, as if by magic, in the eye of the wind. It was as if a modern steam fleet was engaged with a squadron of the old-fashioned sailing-vessels, choosing their own distance, and fighting or not fighting, as suited their convenience.

56. "Astonished and confounded, as well by the manœuvring as by the rapidity of the English fire, the Spanish officers could not refuse their admiration. They knew they were inferior at sea, but had not fully realized their inferiority, notwithstanding the lessons Drake, Hawkins,

Cavendish, and others had already taught them. But here were the English firing four shots to their one, while their ships were so nimble that, with a fresh breeze, even the swiftest of the Spanish ships could not touch them. Such splendid gunners and skillful seamen the Spaniards had never seen before, and were hardly able to believe in their existence."

57. The wind was from the west, so that the English fleet were able to keep to the windward, giving them an increased advantage over their antagonists. The Spanish gunners, drafted from the army, could not manage the naval ordnance, and their shots flew high and scarcely touched the English ships. On the other hand, the Spanish vessels were riddled with shot, and men fell killed and wounded on every side. But the ships were too strongly built to be easily destroyed, and so the monsters continued to receive fearful blows, and sailed wearily and helplessly on. Toward night, Medina Sidonia, finding it impossible to bring on a general engagement, signaled to make sail up the Channel, the rear to be covered by the squadron under his second in command, Don Martinez de Recaldi.

58. "The wind was now rising and promised a squally evening. The English ships withdrew for want of powder. An express was sent up to London for a fresh supply. A fast boat was dispatched to Lord Harry Seymour, who commanded a fleet of coasters farther up the Channel, with a letter reporting progress so far, and bidding him be on the alert. But the misfortunes of the Spaniards were not yet over. The Capitana, one of their largest galleons, fouled with another vessel and broke her bowsprit. She fell behind, and was left to her fate. In the morning Drake took possession of her, and found many casks of reals, and, what was of more importance, some

tons of gunpowder, with which the Roebuck, the swiftest traveler of the fleet, flew to the lord admiral.

59. "Shortly after dark another serious accident occurred. The officers of one of the great galleons, impatient and irritated at the results of the action, were quarreling with one another. The captain struck the master-gunner with a stick. The gunner, who was from Holland, went below in a rage, thrust a burning linstock, or long match, into a powder-barrel, and sprang through a port-hole into the sea. The deck was blown off from stem to stern. Two hundred seamen and soldiers were sent into the air: some fell into the water and were drowned; some, scorched or mutilated, dropped back into the wreck. The ship, which was one of the largest in the fleet, was built so strongly that she survived the shock, and at daylight the English took possession of her. At the bottom of the hold were many barrels of powder, which Lord Howard so sorely needed."

THE PROGRESS OF THE FIGHT.

60. On the morning of July 22d the Spanish admiral saw the remainder of the English fleet coming up from Plymouth Harbor, and he made all sail up the Channel. Owing to the want of powder, the attack of the English was less vigorous than on the day before, but still they dogged the Spaniards in the most persevering manner, and succeeded in inflicting serious damage upon many of the Spanish vessels. The breeze from the west still continued, but it was light, and the fleets made but little headway during the day.

61. On Tuesday, July 23d, a strong morning breeze sprang up from the east, and the Spaniards found themselves for the first time to the windward. Taking advan-

tage of the situation, they bore down upon the English fleet, and tried to bring on a general engagement. This challenge the English would not accept, and stood out to sea toward the west. The Spaniards thought they were retreating, and gave chase. All the galleons were bad sailers, but some were better than others, and soon the San Marcus outstripped her consorts. When several miles ahead of all her companions the wind shifted to the west, leaving the English to the windward. Lord Howard immediately bore down in his flag-ship, the Ark, and attacked the San Marcus, but she defended herself with great bravery, and for an hour and a half fought single-handed, delivering eighty shots and receiving five hundred. His powder again giving out, Lord Howard was obliged to withdraw. This action was fought off Plymouth Harbor, so that in the three days' fight the Armada had made no substantial progress toward its destination.

62. "By this time the news that the Armada was in the Channel had circulated throughout the length and breadth of England, and from every creek and port and harbor came accession of goodly ships, equipped at the cost of leading squires and nobles, and manned by her 'best blood.' From Lyme and Weymouth and Poole and the Isle of Wight, young lords and gentlemen came streaming out in every smack or sloop they could lay hold of, to snatch their share of danger and glory at Howard's side. The strength which they were able to add was little or nothing, but they brought enthusiasm; they brought to the half-starved crews the sense that the heart of all England was with them, and this assurance transformed every seaman into a hero.

63. "On Tuesday evening, after the fight, Medina Sidonia counted a hundred sail behind him, and he ob-

served, with some uneasiness, that the numbers were continually increasing. On Wednesday, July 24th, the weather was calm, and the English lay idle at a short distance from the Armada waiting for powder.

64. "Thursday, July 25th, was the feast-day of Spain's patron saint, St. Jago; of him who, mounted on a milk-white steed, had ridden in fore-front of battle in one of the Spanish encounters with the Moors, and had led them to victory. Should nothing on this holy day be done in his honor by those whom he had so greatly favored? It was decided to make an attack. The galleys led the way, and in their van rode three of the four great galliasses, thrashing the sea to foam with three hundred oars apiece. The English met them with such tremendous discharges of chain-shot that, had not the wind risen about noon, enabling the Spanish ships to come up to their assistance, the galleys would surely have been taken. When the lord admiral withdrew his ships, the Spaniards were so cowed that they made no attempt to pursue them."

65. "Thus," says Canon Kingsley, "the fight had thundered on the live-long afternoon, beneath the virgin cliffs of Freshwater, on the Isle of Wight, while myriad sea-fowl rose screaming from every ledge, and with their black wings spotted the snow-white walls of chalk; and the lone shepherd hurried down the slopes above to peer over the dizzy ledge, and forgot the wheat-ear fluttering in his snare, while, trembling, he gazes upon glimpses of tall masts and gorgeous flags, piercing at times the league-broad veil of sulphur-smoke which weltered far below."

BRIEF RESPITE FROM BATTLE.

66. Friday, July 26th, was a tranquil summer day. The wind died away, and the two fleets, but a few miles

apart, lay rocking on the waves. The Duke of Medina Sidonia took advantage of the pause and sent a swift messenger to the Prince of Parma, praying him to dispatch to his assistance forty small sailing-vessels, capable of contending with the light swift craft of the English. All the next day, July 27th, the two fleets sailed slowly up the Channel in hostile but silent companionship—the Spaniard convinced he could not meet the Englishman in open fight; the Englishman heedful that he should not be surrounded by a superior force. At night the battered and maltreated Armada took refuge in the harbor of Calais.

67. The same afternoon Lord Howard was joined by Sir Harry Seymour with his squadron of sixteen vessels, which had been keeping watch along the eastern ports, and the combined fleet dropped anchor to the eastward of Calais, and within a mile and a half of the French shore. "Never, since England was England," says Mr. Motley, "had such a sight been seen as now revealed itself in those narrow straits between Dover and Calais. Along that low, sandy shore, and quite within the range of the Calais fortifications, one hundred and thirty Spanish ships—the greater number of them the largest and most heavily armed in the world—lay face to face, and scarcely out of cannon-shot, with one hundred and fifty English sloops and frigates, the strongest and swiftest that the island could furnish, and commanded by men whose exploits had rung through the world.

68. "Farther along the coast, invisible but known to be performing a most perilous and vital service, was a squadron of Dutch vessels of all sizes lining both the outer and inner of the sand-banks of the Flemish coasts and swarming in all the estuaries and inlets of that intricate and dangerous cruising-ground between Dunkirk and

Texel. Those fleets of Holland and Zealand, numbering some one hundred and fifty galleons, sloops, and fly-boats, lay patiently blockading every possible egress from the ports in possession of the Duke of Parma, and longing to grapple with him as soon as his fleet of gunboats and hoys, packed with his Spanish and Italian veterans, should venture to set forth upon the sea for their long-meditated enterprise."

69. This friendly attitude of the Dutch to the English was due to a variety of causes. Both nations represented the new religion in its struggle against the established church. In consequence of the terrible atrocities of the Duke of Alva, the Dutch had an inextinguishable hatred for the Spaniards, and were ready to do anything to thwart their plans and diminish their power. Then, too, the Dutch remembered how the ships of Elizabeth, laden with provisions, had brought succor to their beleaguered cities and saved the lives of their famished people. So, animated by enmity on the one side and by gratitude on the other, the Dutch for a time forgot their struggle for maritime supremacy with the English, and brought all their force to bear to support the English cause in its hour of greatest need.

70. The Spaniards seem never to have anticipated this energetic action on the part of the Dutch. The Duke of Medina Sidonia now found that he could get no direct sea communication with the Spanish land-forces; and the Duke of Parma found himself in a situation where his invincible army was powerless, and his soldierly experience and talents were of no avail. The plans of the Spanish admiral to make use of the small vessels of Parma had been thwarted by the Dutch, and the dispersion of the Dutch vessels had been prevented by the fierce attack of Howard and Drake upon the Armada.

71. In coming to anchor on that Saturday night in Calais Harbor, however, the Spaniards had gained two important points. Their ships were under the protection of friendly land-batteries; and nothing remained to prevent the co-operation of the land-forces and the fleet. The Duke of Parma could march his forces westward and embark from Calais instead of Dunkirk, and thus turn the flank of the Dutch fleet.

72. Sunday, July 29th, was a day of suspense and anxiety on the part of both the contending forces. The English knew that a junction with Parma was now possible, and Howard and Drake were too good seamen not to know that, in a close and general engagement, the superior size, weight, and numbers of the Spanish ships would prevail. On the other hand, the Spaniards knew that they were in an unsafe harbor should a strong wind spring up from the west, and Medina Sidonia began to have a wholesome dread of the valor and strength which guarded the homes of Britain. The day passed in Sabbath quiet and repose, and when the sun set there was no indication that a night's strife was to follow, potential as shaping the future destinies of both Spain and England.

FRIGHT AND FLIGHT.

73. During the day, Captain Winter, of the English fleet, suggested that the Spaniards might be driven from their anchorage by fire-ships, and his plan was adopted. Six vessels were loaded with wild-fire, rosin, pitch, brimstone, and other combustibles, and made ready to sail. The night was dark, with indications in sky and sea of a coming gale. "When the Spanish bells," says Froude, "were about striking twelve, and, save the watch on deck, soldiers and seamen lay stretched in sleep, certain dark

objects, which had been seen dimly drifting in the tide near where the galleons lay thickest, shot suddenly into pyramids of light, flames leaping from ruddy sail to sail, flickering on the ropes and forecastles, masts and bowsprits, a lurid blaze of conflagration.

74. "A cool commander might have ordered out his boats and towed the fire-ships clear; but Medina Sidonia, with a strain already upon him beyond the strength of his capacity, saw coming some terrible engine of destruction, like the floating mine which had shattered Parma's bridge at Antwerp. Panic spread through the entire Armada. Hasty and impetuous cries arose on board each menaced vessel. 'Up anchors, comrades! Out every stitch of canvas! Away, away! for in the track of those blazing ships follow death and ruin!'

75. "There are times when immense bodies of men suddenly give way to the influence of a needless but overmastering panic, and this was one of them. Every cable was cut; galleon, galliasse, and patache drove hurriedly through the press of shipping, each heedless of its comrade's danger, and seeking frantically some channel of escape. In vain the Duke of Medina Sidonia attempted to reform his disordered array. So long as the darkness lasted, the confusion prevailed; and ship after ship reeled, staggered, and drifted out to sea. Several of the Spanish ships were disabled, two were burned, and it was not until they found themselves six miles from shore, and at a secure distance from the smoldering hulks, that they recovered from their terror."

RENEWAL OF THE FIGHT.

76. On Monday, July 29th, when the day dawned, Lord Howard discovered the Spanish fleet in great disor-

der, scattered over a wide space in the Channel. He immediately ordered an advance, and, while Drake made a bold attack upon the main body of the enemy, the lord high admiral drove upon the sands several of the sluggard vessels of the Armada which the fire-ships had failed to drive out to sea. For several hours he engaged the great galliasse under the direct command of Admiral Moncada, which was aground upon the sands. The vessel was captured and Moncada slain, and the English admiral hastened to the assistance of Drake.

77. "It was well," says Froude, "that no more time was wasted over so small a matter. Lord Howard had already delayed too long for his fame. It was no time for the admiral of the fleet to be loitering over a stray feather which had dropped from the enemy's plume when every ship was imperiously needed for a far more important service. Medina Sidonia intended to return to Calais, but his ships had drifted in the night far to the east, and before his signal of return could be obeyed the English fleet was upon them.

78. "Sir Henry Seymour, with his sixteen ships, having the advantage of wind, speed, and skill, came upon a cluster of Spanish galleons at eight in the morning. Reserving their fire till within a hundred and twenty yards, and wasting no cartridges, the English ships continued through the entire forenoon to pour upon them one continuous rain of shot. They were driven together, and became entangled in a confused and helpless mass.

79. "Drake, in the mean time, had fallen upon a score of galleons under the direct command of Medina Sidonia himself. They were better handled than the rest, and were endeavoring to keep sea-room and retain some command of themselves. But their wretched sailing powers put them to a disadvantage, for which no skill or courage

could compensate. The English were always at windward of them; and, hemmed in at every turn, they, too, were forced back upon their consorts, hunted together as a shepherd hunts sheep upon a common, and the whole mass of them were forced slowly eastward, away from the only harbor open to them, and into the unknown waters of the North Sea.

80. "Howard came up at noon to join in the work of destruction. The Spaniards' gun-practice, always bad, was helpless beyond all past experience. From eight o'clock in the morning until sunset the English, almost untouched themselves, fired into them without intermission at short range. They ceased only when the last cartridge was spent, and every man was weary with labor. They took no prizes, and they attempted to take none. Their orders were to sink and destroy. They saw three great galleons go down, and three more drift toward the sands, where their destruction was certain.

81. "On board the Spanish ships all was consternation and despair. Toward sunset the great Santa Maria went down with all on board. When the ships' companies were called over, it was discovered that no less than four thousand men had been killed or drowned, and twice as many wounded. The survivors were so utterly dispirited that nothing could induce them to face England's sea-kings again."

CHASE AND DESTRUCTION.

82. On Tuesday afternoon, July 30th, Lord Howard summoned a council of war, which decided upon a course of action. Lord Henry Seymour with his squadron was to return to guard the mouth of the Thames against any attempt on the part of Parma, while the remainder of the fleet was to continue the chase of the Armada. Ninety

vessels, under Howard, Drake, and Frobisher, followed the flying Spaniards into the North Sea. "We have the army of Spain before us," Drake wrote, "and hope, with the grace of God, to wrestle a fall with him. There was never anything pleased me better than seeing the enemy flying with a southerly wind to the northward. God grant you have a good eye to the Duke of Parma, for, if we live, I doubt not to handle the matter with the Duke of Sidonia, as he shall wish himself at St. Mary's Port, among his orange-trees!"

83. The wind, now strong from the south, had risen to a gale. The Spanish ships, so fashioned as to sail only before the wind, were driven northward. Between them and the shore, where lay possible safety, was the dreadful English fleet, which had battered them so sorely during the past ten days. Before them was the sea, full of unknown perils. "Not only man but God was against them. *His* wind blew discomfiture to their meditated enterprise. More than one poor, crippled ship dropped behind as her spars snapped, or the water made its way through her wounded seams in the straining seas. The Spaniards, stricken with a wonderful fear, made no attempt to succor their consorts, but pressed heavily on, leaving them to founder."

84. The pursuit continued until Friday, August 2d. There was now no more danger to be apprehended from the scattered enemy. The wind was threatening, and, the supply of provisions beginning to fail, Howard and Drake determined on returning homeward, leaving a couple of pinnaces to dog the Spaniards past the Scottish isles. Though the wind was contrary, they beat back against it without loss, and in four or five days the vessels, with their half-starved crews, all safely arrived in Margate Roads, having done the noblest service that fleet ever rendered to a country in the hour of supreme peril.

85. "Meanwhile, so much as remained of the Invincible Armada was buffeted to and fro by the resistless gale, like a shuttlecock between two invisible players. The monster left its bones on the iron-bound shore of Norway and on the granite cliffs of the Hebrides. Its course could be traced by its wrecks. Day followed day, and still God's wrath endured. On the 5th of August Admiral Oguendo, in his flag-ship, together with one of the great galliasses and thirty-eight other vessels, were driven by the fury of the tempest upon the rocks and reefs of Ireland, and nearly every soul on board perished. Of one hundred and thirty-four vessels which, gay with gold and amid triumphal shouts and loud music, had sailed from Corunna July 12th, only fifty-three battered and useless hulks returned to the ports of Spain."

86. The fate and exploits of the Armada are graphically summed up in the emphatic language of Sir Francis Drake. "It is happily manifested," he says, "indeed, to all nations how their navy which they termed *invincible*, consisting of nearly one hundred and forty sail of ships, were by thirty of her Majesty's ships of war, and a few of our own merchants, by the wise and advantageous conduct of Lord Charles Howard, High Admiral of England, beaten and shuffled together from Lizard in Cornwall to Portland, from Portland to Calais; and from Calais, driven by squibs from their anchors, were chased out of sight of England, round about Scotland and Ireland. With all their great and terrible ostentation, they did not, in all their sailing round about England, so much as sink or take one ship, bark, pinnace, or cock-boat of ours, or even burn so much as one sheep-cote on the land."

CHAPTER VIII.

FREEDOM'S VOYAGE TO AMERICA.

DISSENT AND PERSECUTION.

1. THROUGH the middle ages England, like the rest of the world, had been in full communion with the Church of Rome. When the Reformation had swept over Europe and left dissent to crystallize into various Protestant sects, England too had dissented, and her king had established the Anglican Church. This church, when it assumed final form, had for its supreme head, not the pope, but the king, and under him the clergy held their offices. The Roman Catholic ritual was not, as in some of the European sects, entirely given up, but was modified to suit the new order. And when the change was effected, the new ministers firm in their positions, the new service-books ready for use, then the Catholics were summarily ordered to embrace the reformed faith.

2. At that time it had not dawned upon the world that there might be more than one way to worship God in truth. Catholics honestly believed that Protestants were going straight to perdition, and Protestants as honestly believed that a like fate was in store for the pope and his followers. When this was the temper of conviction, the natural thing for each church to do was to perse-

cute every other; not from hate, but from the benevolent determination to oblige men to accept the true religion and save their souls, even though it might be necessary in the course of proceedings to burn their bodies. Mixed with this legitimate missionary spirit were all sorts of political motives. The church, whether Catholic or Protestant, was closely connected with the state, and through all the corruptions of party politics religion had to be dragged.

3. So, when the English state established Protestantism, its first duty and interest was to suppress Catholicism. After two Protestant kings, a Catholic queen came to the throne, and with her the Protestants fell and the Catholics rose. The former were forbidden their service, their ministers were turned out of their positions; fines, imprisonment, burning punished those who held out against the "true faith." Again the scene changed. The queen died, and by her Protestant successor freedom of worship was denied to Catholics, and the Anglican Church was re-established as the Church of England.

4. Meantime, in the Church of England a spirit of criticism had grown up. Stricter thinkers disliked the imposing ceremonies which the English church still retained: some of the ministers ceased to wear gowns in preaching, performed the marriage ceremony without using a ring, and were in favor of simplifying all the church service. Unpretentious workers began to tire of the everlasting quarreling, and to long for a religion simple and quiet. These soon met trouble, for the rulers had decided that salvation was by the Church of England, as the sovereign, its head, should order. Dissent was the two-fold guilt of heresy and revolution—sin against God and crime against the king and English law. They were forbidden to preach at all if they would not

wear a gown during service, and the people who went to hear them were punished. This treatment caused serious thought among the "non-conformists," as they were called, and, once thinking, they soon concluded that the king had no such supreme right to order the church, and the church had over its ministers no such right of absolute dictation.

5. Various sects sprang up, called by various names, differing among themselves upon minor points, but agreeing more or less in dissent from the full, unquestioned rule and service of the Episcopal Church. Against all these dissenters the laws acted as against the Catholics. Not only must Englishmen be Protestants, they must be Protestants of the Church of England. Bodies were organized to keep strict watch of the non-conformists. They were forbidden their simpler church worship and fined if they did not attend that of the English Church. They were "scoffed and scorned by the profane multitude, and so vexed, as truly their affliction was not small."

JOHN ROBINSON'S CONGREGATION.

6. Among that division of the non-conformists called Puritans was a little congregation at Scrooby, a town in north England. The pastor was John Robinson, wise, kind, dignified, scholarly; and his helper in church work and government was Elder William Brewster, a college man who had served at the royal court. For the rest, the congregation were mainly Bible-reading farmers, who wished only to live in peace according to Bible teaching. Royal servants were watchful, and an open church was out of the question; but every Sunday they met for service wherever they could, sometimes in Elder Brewster's big house, sometimes out-doors, anywhere so that they

might listen to their beloved pastor. During the week they worked their farms, thinking and talking of the iniquities of the Catholics, the impurities of the Episcopalians, the hard ways that beset the Puritans, and the righteous God who looked down upon it all to record and avenge.

7. Quiet as such a simple church in a corner of England must have been, it was not left undisturbed. Priests of the dominant church and officers of the civil service soon pounced down with the demand that the Puritan farmers stop all this "new-fangledness," and return to the ways of the loyal church. John Robinson's people, however, had no notion of giving up their new-fangledness. They possessed a full share of English obstinacy, and, backed in it by their consciences, were not likely to surrender at once. So their troubles began. They "were hunted and persecuted on every side. Some were clapped into prisons, others had their houses beset and watched night and day, and hardly escaped their hands, and the most were fain to fly and leave their houses and habitations and the means of their livelihood."

8. What shall we do? thought the distressed farmers. We can not live in such persecution. We will have to go away. Give up? Indeed, no! We shall not belie our consciences for any man. Since God is behind us, we *will not* conform. And, under opposition and injustice, Puritan lips set themselves rigid, Puritan hearts closed against the persecutors, strong reaction from the beautiful ceremonies and graceful living that could hide such unbrotherliness became almost worship of unloveliness and hardship. In after years the lives of their descendants were shaped into a narrow severity, not drawn from the sweetness and light of the gospel which they read, but from the bitter fountains of their early sufferings and wrongs.

9. What shall we do? cried the harassed farmers. We will have to leave our home and go to Holland, where others like us have already gone, and where, we hear, is freedom of religion for all men. Yet how should they get there? "for, though they could not stay, yet were they not suffered to go." And, if they should get there, how could they, who "had only been used to a plain country life and the innocent trade of husbandry," manage to live in a country where people spoke an outlandish language instead of good English, and earned their money by trade.

10. Somehow God would help. Give up their religion they would not. They set about going. They bribed ship captains, feed the sailors, paid unreasonable rates for passage, and then, deserted by these same captains and sailors, tried it again with others, were betrayed into the hands of officers who rifled them of what money they had left and turned them over to prison. Hard luck! Set free from prison, they bargained with a Dutchman to take them in his ship to Holland, but as they were going aboard a company of armed men surprised them, and the Dutchman, afraid to be seen in such company, hastily sailed away with half the "Pilgrims," leaving the rest terrified on the shore.

11. "Take us back!" cried the men. "Don't you see our wives and children crying after us!" But the Dutchman was afraid of the soldiers. "What will they do without us!" cried the men, straining their eyes to see all that was happening on shore. "Our goods are not yet aboard—take us back!" No use. The Dutchman sailed away, and the soldiers carried off the frightened women and children to prison. When the authorities had them safely locked up, they did not know what to do with silly women and helpless children, who cried for their husbands and fathers, and when asked concern-

ing their homes cried the more and declared they hadn't any; and, after making themselves sufficient trouble, they solved the important problem by letting the ridiculous creatures go again. The Dutchman's ship, through a terrible storm, came to land. The distressed husbands sought the distressed wives, and troublous wanderings ended in reunion. So were they continually thwarted; but, by one means or another, determined wills bent circumstances to their end, and at last they reached Holland.

12. Strangers as they were, destitute, all unused to the new life and people, they had trouble enough at first, but they wasted little time staring at the new world. It was a world they were to become a part of as soon as possible, and, with characteristic earnestness, they fell to work at any thing they found to do. After a year in Amsterdam they settled in Leyden. They made them homes. They learned as best they could the uncouth language. They taught their farmer hands unaccustomed crafts, and applied their farmer heads to the mysteries of trade.

13. Elder Brewster, with the tastes and habits of a gentleman, a rapidly diminishing property, and a large family of children, looked about for work, and presently obtained pupils whom he taught English after an original method. Later he set up a printing-press, and in printing Puritan books, forbidden to be published in England, found plenty to do. Mr. Robinson visited his people and was busy for their welfare, preached, studied, wrote books; he was a kind friend and helper, and a scholar besides, and proud of him were his devoted flock.

14. Leyden Dutchmen looked with curiosity upon the knot of plain foreigners, sober men, quiet women, children named after all the Bible saints and heavenly virtues. Bibles they bought and evidently read. It was rumored

that together every morning and before each meal each household held service of prayer, and long sermons and various devotions wholly filled the Sabbath. Queer people, meditated the Hollanders. But they soon found that it was safe to trust the Bible readers. Though they were peculiar about Sunday, they were surprisingly certain to keep their promises, and for all their propensity to pray without ceasing they made most faithful workmen. Superintendents sought them for laborers, merchants willingly gave them credit; and with the passing years they became settled and quietly prosperous. The Bibles were not neglected, the daily prayers and weekly sermons were methodically attended.

15. The unpretentious people were not unobserved. Many from England came to enjoy like freedom of worship, and far outside of Leyden John Robinson's learning was known. When Arminians and Calvinists fell into hot disputes, and Leyden ministers and university professors held public meetings twice a week to settle knotty points of doctrine, John Robinson was always there, listening eagerly to both sides. Many a famous talk he had with the ministers and professors. We must have Mr. Robinson confute the Arminians, cried his friends among themselves.

16. So on a day the Puritan pastor, somewhat demurring because he was a foreigner, yet withal not loath to ride a tilt with the enemy, confronted Episcopus, the Arminian professor; and it is reported by the Calvinists that his overwhelming arguments utterly nonplussed and put the great Episcopus to rout. Oh, those theological debates! About the paltry affairs of this world it was not right to quarrel. When personal considerations were at stake, Puritan worthies could bridle the tongue; but when was called in question some keenly felt phase of

the truth, some doctrine their precious Bible seemed to teach, then the repressed fire burst into legitimate flame, and righteous indignation with magnificent effect hurled back and forth the thunderbolts of prophecy and psalm.

THE DEPARTURE FROM LEYDEN.

17. After some eleven or twelve years of this life in Leyden the Puritans began to grow restless. Holland was not home to them, and they were lonely. Some of them were growing old, and the somber burden of poverty and exile began to weary the brave shoulders. The children were growing up, and hard work and cramped life pressed all too severely upon the young natures, so that they either threw off the yoke and turned to bad ways or, bearing it patiently, missed the chance of education and grew old before their time. They feared to stay longer in this foreign country lest the children should learn from the Dutch to break the Sabbath, should lose their native language, should cease to be Englishmen.

18. Perhaps it would be best to move again and settle in some land under the flag of dear England—harsh England, that would not grant them peace at home. Though they should have to go to most distant regions, they would cheerfully go, and consider themselves God's missionaries there, if only they might have the protection of England's king. They would go and break the way for others of their countrymen less strong, and in America, if need be, prepare an English home for Englishmen.

19. Gravely the elders talked together. The uncongenial life had been cheerfully borne; a new uprooting and uncertain change would be as steadfastly carried

through, once they were sure God willed it. And at last it seemed best to decide upon removal. "The dangers were great but not desperate, the difficulties were many but not invincible—and all of them, through the help of God, by fortitude and patience, might either be borne or overcome." Sturdy courage! O England, to exile such sons!

20. Where, then, should they go? "I will guide thee," reads the promise of the Puritan's Bible, and to God they turn in prayer for direction. A general meeting is held, and much discussion results in the decision to cross the Atlantic to Virginia, Great Britain's vast new realm. They would not settle near the colony already planted there, for that was of the Episcopal Church and might molest them; but away by themselves somewhere—anywhere, if only they might nestle in a remote corner of their king's dominions, and on English soil be free to follow their own conscience. God and the king was the loyal thought—yet, if there *must* be choice, the king shall not be first.

21. But, sending petition to the king, they found that he would give them no assurance of freedom of worship; it was intimated that, if they did go, the royal eye might be expected to wink at the proceeding; but, as for promises, royalty would not commit itself. Here was a discouragement. How should they dare break up their homes and cross the ocean to an unknown, uncolonized land, with no assurance of protection and liberty when they arrived there? But the leaders rallied again: "If on the king's part there is a purpose or desire to wrong us," they cried, "though we had a seal as broad as the house-floor it would not serve the turn, for there would be means enough found to recall or reverse it. . . . We must rest herein on God's providence, as we have done

before." Not lacking in comprehension of the world's ways and in canny shrewdness were those Puritans!

22. Wearisome negotiations then began with men who should furnish means for the removal. Back and forth, from Leyden to London, from London to Leyden, the agents went; letters passed from Robinson and Brewster to the London merchants, and from the London merchants back. Poor Robert Cushman, agent for the Puritans, experienced numerous tribulations; pushed by the merchants to make an agreement, blamed by his friends for going beyond his instructions, his letters defending himself give a spirited glimpse into the harrowed soul of a quick-tempered Christian.

23. After months of all this, the arrangements were concluded. A body of London merchants agreed to furnish ships and provisions for the passage, on certain conditions: for seven years after landing the Puritans were to hold all property in common; they were to fish, plant, build, and at the end of seven years were to share with the merchants, according to certain specified conditions, the accumulated property, capital, and profits. Hard terms! But they could not choose, and go they must.

24. Who should go? This question agitated the Leyden congregation. Not all could take the voyage. Perhaps not all cared to: it was so far, so far! Yet the most were willing, and it remained to select from the large congregation those most fit for the hard task. There was dividing of friend from friend, of husband from wife, of father from child. Elder Brewster would go as their spiritual leader, since the beloved pastor must for the present stay with those who remained, hoping later to cross the sea and come to them.

25. A ship, the Speedwell, was fitted up in Holland;

another, the Mayflower, awaited them in England. When all was ready they appointed a day of solemn fasting and prayer. Pastor Robinson preached to them "a good part of the day" on the text, "And there at the river, by Ahava, I proclaimed a fast, that we might humble ourselves before our God and seek of him a right way for us and for our children and for all our substance," and "the rest of the time was spent in pouring out prayers to the Lord with great fervency mixed with abundance of tears." Again they met together in a "feast" at the pastor's house. Sorry feasting!

26. The hospitality was large, but hearts were too full for much but tears: a tender, painful farewell gathering, their white-haired pastor going about among them with words of comfort and counsel, gentle last suggestions, scripture texts believed, though the voice that repeats them trembles and breaks—believed and clung to through the tug of parting. "Fear thou not, for I am with thee. Be not dismayed, for I am thy God. I will strengthen thee; yea, I will help thee; yea, I will uphold thee with the right hand of my righteousness!" "God is our refuge and strength, a very present help in trouble. Therefore will not we fear, though the earth be removed and though the mountains be carried into the midst of the sea. The Lord of hosts is with us; the God of Jacob is our refuge." Yes, they believed. And believing, they sang through tears—quivering pain notes at first, then, faith dominating, the tones grew firmer and sustained, until the final words rang out clear and strong; and with the end of the hymn they were ready for last earnest hand-clasps and quiet good-night.

27. To take ship, they went to Delft Haven, fourteen miles from Leyden, and to the port Pastor Robinson, with most of their friends, accompanied them. One

more night on land, then the long voyage and the uncertain future. There was little sleep that night; and again, with Bible words and Christian counsel, hearts were strengthened.

28. In the morning, the wind being fair, "they went aboard and their friends with them, where truly doleful was the sight of that sad and mournful parting, to see what sighs and sobs and prayers did sound among them." We know, we know—God *is* our refuge—but sore is the parting. We *are* willing—but our hearts are wrung. There is no thought of regret or turning—but oh, the pain of it! The Dutchmen, loitering in the sunshine on the shore, watching with heavy curiosity this strange departure, suddenly find their own eyes filled with sympathetic tears. We must be off! cries the captain, half impatient over so much fervency and tears. They kneel around the pastor, and, with unsteady voice, though his trust is firm, he calls upon the God in whom they believe to guide and bless these his children. Once more the arms cling close. Mother, mother, how can I let you go! My child, my child!—Beloved, you will come over to me soon. Oh, my husband!—God wills it; I must go. My son, I shall not live to see your face again.—Loosen the clasping arms; unfold the clinging fingers. You stay and we go, and the ocean lies between. The wind comes breathing, the sails fill; good-by! good-by! across the widening space—and they are gone.

THE VOYAGE.

29. They sailed first to meet the Mayflower and others of the Puritan company at Southampton, England. There they called Robert Cushman to account, fell out with one of their London patrons, read together an affec-

tionate farewell letter from Mr. Robinson, made all final arrangements for the voyage, and on August 5th, 1620, set sail in the two ships for America. But the captain of the Speedwell, half-hearted in the business, twice had them back to land to repair pretended leaks; and the second time, putting in at Plymouth, it was determined to leave the Speedwell and a part of the Puritan band. The little company, small enough before, was again reduced, "like Gideon's army." Some were discouraged with the many hindrances and willingly stayed; some were begining to fear for the success of the voyage, undertaken so late in the season; some were weak, and could be spared where there was need of the strongest; some little children were sent back to await a later passage; Robert Cushman, vexed to the soul by the unsatisfactoriness of his negotiations, sick and disheartened, stayed behind. Again there were sad parting, tears, and prayers; but God would sustain, and, leaving the companion ship and the last friends, the Mayflower sailed from Plymouth, September 6th.

30. One hundred and two "Pilgrims," seeking a better country: men, women, children, servants and handmaidens. Elder William Brewster with his wife Mary, his two sons Love and Wrestling, and a boy, Richard More; the Winslows, with two men-servants and Richard More's little sister Ellen; William Bradford and his wife Dorothy, their only child being left behind; the Allertons, the Martins, the Whites, with their son Resolved; Mr. and Mrs. Mullins with their children Joseph and Priscilla, and a servant; Mr. Hopkins and his family; Mr. Warren, lonely enough without the wife and children left behind; John Billington, his wife Ellen, and his two sons; the two Tilley families, with their cousins Henry Samson and Humility Cooper, children whose

parents were not with them; Mr. Cook and John his son, his wife and other children being in England yet; John Rigdale and Alice his wife; Miles Standish, bold English soldier, with Rose his wife; John Alden, the cooper, "a hopeful young man and much desired"; Thomas Tinker, with his wife and child; these and many others in the little ship sailed over the wide ocean in search of an English home where Englishmen might freely worship God.

31. The voyage at first was fair enough. They were seasick, some of them; the children had to be watched lest they fall overboard; a profane bully of a sailor, after using all manner of abuse toward the sick ones, himself fell ill and died, "And," says William Bradford, recording it, "thus his curses light on his own head, and it was an astonishment to all his fellows, for they noted it to be the just hand of God upon him." Later came storms and danger, with breaking of masts, eager consultation among the ship's officers, water, wind, confusion; but the masts were mended and they "committed themselves to the will of God and resolved to proceed." Big John Howland, coming on deck, was thrown into the sea by a lurch of the ship, but with a rope was hauled in again and saved. Before they came to land a little boy was born in the Hopkins family, and they named him Oceanus; and Samuel Fuller's servant, a young man named William Butten, died as they neared the coast.

32. The hard voyage was over at last, and on the 9th of November Cape Cod appeared. They knew about Cape Cod from the map and book of Captain John Smith, who had tried to plant a colony there some years before, but they intended to land somewhere near the Hudson River, and turned south along the coast. Shoals and breakers barring their passage that way, they returned,

and, on November 11th, anchored in Cape Cod harbor. "Being now passed the vast ocean and a sea of troubles, before their preparation unto further proceedings . . . they fell down upon their knees and blessed the Lord, the God of Heaven, who had brought them over the vast and furious ocean, and delivered them from all perils and miseries thereof, again to set their feet on the firm and stable earth, their proper element."

33. So there they were, and as yet no one had left the ship. It was winter. The cold blue ocean beat the cold white shore, and the dark forest further back rustled and moaned in the north wind, whistling bleak welcome. What could those women and children do there? West from the sea lay an unexplored country, no one knew how large; dark forest uninhabited, save for the dusky Indian, clothed the land in an unbroken mystery of wilderness; north and south stretched the desolate coast, stretched five hundred miles ere it reached the nearest European settlement; east lay the ocean, not to be recrossed. How could the men build shelter in the midst of a northern winter? And they must build, for the ship's store of provisions was none too large, and the captain impatient to be off again before famine set in. After ages of comfort—shiver to think of it!—that lone, cold landing; the stretching, desolate coast; the cutting, wind-blown snow; the little anchored ship, bearing treasure of warm human hearts, strong human wills, clear purpose, courage untamed. Slight protection, the rocking ship, for such precious store of life, with that white, relentless winter coming down upon the bay.

34. The day of casting anchor, those steadfast, earnest men, whose God was the Lord, and whose king was James of England, gathered in the Mayflower cabin and, by a formal statement written and signed, formed them-

selves into a civil state. Note the words of the compact: "In the name of God, amen. We, whose names are underwritten, the loyal subjects of our dread sovereign lord, King James—" have fled over seas from English persecution? No—"have undertaken, for the glory of God and the advancement of the Christian faith, and honor of our king and country, a voyage to plant the first colony in the northern parts of Virginia." God and the king; true Christians and true Englishmen. The document reads with a calm dignity, a clear political instinct, a solemn religious faith, worthy of Englishmen. They may have braved English laws for conscience' sake, but there is no bravado; they may keenly feel the injustice they have experienced, but there was no repining.

35. Then began expeditions to the land. The men, under Captain Standish, went in parties in a small boat, returning to the ship at night, or, in some cases, they camped on the shore and were away from the ship several days. Wading to the shore through water too shallow even for the small boat, with sea-spray freezing as it covered them, tramping through the snow, breaking through the forest, with prayer each morning, and always a day of rest on Sunday, they explored the coast and wilderness for the best place to settle. They found yellow Indian corn buried by the Indians in sand-heaps, and carried it to the ship, counting it God's special providence that they were thus provided with seed to plant the next year. "The Lord is never wanting unto his in their greatest needs; let his holy Name have all the praise!" cried William Bradford. November wore away, dark and wild, and with set teeth December came. Back and forth went the exploring parties. A skirmish with the Indians took place; but "it pleased God to vanquish their enemies and give them deliverance, and by his spe-

cial providence so to dispose, that not any one of them was hurt or hit, though their arrows came close." Thereupon they gave the Lord solemn thanks, and named the place "The First Encounter."

36. After a stormy, dangerous week, Saturday, December 9th, dawned clear, and the sun shone down on the snowy world. The Sabbath day the explorers observed on shore, and Monday they "sounded the harbor and found it fit for shipping, and marched into the land and found a . . . place fit for situation; at least, it was the best they could find, and the season and their present necessity made them glad to accept of it. So they returned to their ship again with this news to the rest of their people, which did much comfort their hearts." This day, December 11th, old style, corresponding to December 21st, new style, is celebrated as the date of the "landing of the Pilgrims."

37. Meantime, what of those left in the ship these four dreary weeks? The ways of life went on in births and deaths; six of the wanderers found the door of the other world; and Peregrine White came into this—first-born of New England. The little boy Jasper More, who came in care of the Carvers, died; and Dorothy Bradford fell overboard and was drowned while her husband was exploring the coast. The men had terrible coughs and colds from wading through the freezing sea, and the women were beginning to suffer from the hardship of it all. The children, child-like, adapted themselves to the situation. Mr. Billington being gone to the shore, his son John, with the family gun well loaded, took occasion to try his skill by shooting it off in the cabin; "yet, by God's mercy, no harm was done!"

38. Midwinter, and provisions low. Seven already buried in the ocean. Sickness setting in with more sever-

ity, women and children to be somehow cared for, two tiny babies to be shielded from all harm, their only home the inhospitable shore. No time to lose! The 16th they began to build the first house, and so was planted Plymouth.

39. In that dead winter time sprang Plymouth. Cold for the seed of the Mayflower, but Mayflower's seed did not easily die. The houses went up, one after another, and as it became possible the company on the ship were transferred to the land. The ship, indeed, became more and more undesirable: sickness prevailed; the sailors did not escape, but dragged about or tossed in their beds in fierce impatience, and, of the Puritans, half their number died before the end of March. Elder Brewster and strong Miles Standish, with half-a-dozen others who were left in health, toiled night and day, cooking, building fires, making beds, washing clothes, adapting their masculine hands to women's offices as they dressed and undressed the feverish patients, cared for the babies whose mothers lay ill, heard the children say their prayers. Ah, Miles Standish, rough captain, nowhere do you stand out braver than against that background! And Rose, thy wife, Rose Standish too must die, ere ever she comes to the home on the shore.

40. The winter wears on. The Indians come to investigate, later to treat with the English. Since there are few well enough to build, the little settlement, snowbound between the ocean and the forest, grows but slowly. Sometimes deaths come twice and thrice in a day, and the whole scene is a funeral and the ocean one black grave. Yet they bear it all patiently, silently: it is the hand of the Lord. Priscilla Mullins sees her father, her mother, her brother, buried in the heartless sea, and stands in the New World alone. "God is our refuge and strength, a very present help in trouble." Priscilla can

bear it as a brave woman will, and, later, finds protection in the strong arms of John Alden. Mr. Winslow watches the waves close over the form of his wife. "My life is spent with sorrow and my years with sighing, . . . but I trusted in thee, O Lord; my times are in thy hand." He can bear it as a brave man can, and not many months after finds comfort in taking to himself the widow of Mr. White; the two knit together by common sorrow and danger. Elizabeth Tilley loses father and mother. John Rigdale and Alice, his wife, die together. Thomas Tinker, wife, and child, all die there in the ship. And the north wind beat the sea and blew through the bare trees. Desolate, desolate welcome! "From the end of the earth will I cry unto thee, when my heart is overwhelmed: lead me to the rock that is higher than I. The rock of my strength and my refuge is in God." They could bear it and be brave; and they did, until God sent the spring with new health for his people.

41. Warmer shines the sun, and April comes. All the people—all whom death has left—are in the houses now, and the Mayflower is ready for the home voyage. They gather at the shore to see the last of her, and send last messages back to the dear home land. Back goes the ship, straight to Old England; yet, with that fearful winter freezing in their memories, scarce fifty of them left to found the lonely settlement, weak yet and worn, not one returns to the easier life at home. The Mayflower disappears on the eastern horizon; the last watcher by the shore is satisfied that she is gone; and then alone, self-governed, self-dependent, free, the sea and wilderness circling close about them, God their Father watching overhead, the Puritans take up their stern life, and in America create New England,

Ellen Coit Brown.

LANDING OF THE PILGRIMS:

42. The breaking waves dashed high
 On a stern and rock-bound coast,
And the woods, against a stormy sky,
 Their giant branches tossed.

43. And the heavy night hung dark
 The woods and waters o'er,
When a band of exiles moored their bark
 On the wild New England shore.

44. Not as the conqueror comes,
 They, the true-hearted, came;
Not with the roll of the stirring drums,
 And the trumpet that speaks of fame;

45. Not as the flying come,
 In silence and in fear—
They shook the depths of the desert's gloom
 With their hymns of lofty cheer.

46. Amidst the storm they sang;
 And the stars heard, and the sea;
And the sounding aisles of the dim woods rang
 To the anthem of the free!

47. The ocean eagle soared
 From his nest by the white wave's foam.
And the rocking pines of the forest roared—
 This was their welcome home.

Mrs. Hemans.

Landing of the Pilgrims.

THE PILGRIM FATHERS.

48. Behold! they come—those sainted forms,
Unshaken through the strife of storms;
Heaven's winter cloud hangs coldly down,
And earth puts on its rudest frown;
But colder, ruder, was the hand
That drove them from their own fair land;
Their own fair land—Refinement's chosen seat,
Art's trophied dwelling, Learning's green retreat;
By Valor guarded and by Victory crowned,
For all but gentle Charity renowned.

49. With streaming eye, yet steadfast heart,
Even from that land they dared to part,
And burst each tender tie;
Haunts, where their sunny youth was passed,
Homes, where they fondly hoped at last
In peaceful age to die.
Friends, kindred, comfort, all they spurned,
Their fathers' hallowed graves,
And to a world of darkness turned,
Beyond a world of waves.

50. When Israel's race from bondage fled,
Signs from on high the wanderers led;
But here—Heaven hung no symbol here,
Their steps to guide, their souls to cheer;
They saw, through sorrow's lengthening night,
Naught but the fagot's guilty light;
The cloud they gazed at was the smoke.
Nor power above, nor power below,
Sustained them in their hour of woe;
A fearful path they trod,

And dared a fearful doom;
To build an altar to their God,
And find a quiet tomb.

51. Yet, strong in weakness, there they stand
On yonder ice-bound rock,
Stern and resolved, that faithful band,
To meet Fate's rudest shock.
Though anguish rends the father's breast,
For them, his dearest and his best,
With him the waste who trod—
Though tears that freeze the mother sheds
Upon her children's houseless heads—
The Christian turns to God.

52. In grateful adoration now
Upon the barren sands they bow.
What tongue of joy e'er woke such prayer
As bursts in desolation there?
What arm of strength e'er wrought such power
As waits to crown that feeble hour?
When into life an infant empire springs,
There falls the iron from the soul,
There Liberty's young accents roll
Up to the King of kings!

53. Spread out earth's holiest record here,
Of days and deeds to reverence dear;
A zeal like this, what pious legends tell?
On kingdoms built
In blood and guilt,
The worshipers of vulgar triumph dwell:
But what exploit with them shall page
Who rose to bless their kind—

Who left their nation and their age
Man's spirit to unbind?
Who boundless seas passed o'er,
And boldly met in every path,
Famine, and frost, and heathen wrath,
To dedicate a shore
Where Piety's meek train might breathe their vow,
And seek their Maker with an unshamed brow;
Where Liberty's glad race might come,
And set up there an everlasting home!

Charles Sprague.

CHAPTER IX.

PLASSEY; AND HOW AN EMPIRE WAS WON.

1. INDIA, the great peninsula stretching from the Himalayas to Cape Comorin, is nearly half as large as Europe, and contains a population of 150,000,000. Myth and tradition claim for this people a very great antiquity, and there are many evidences that in arts, government, and literature, India is at least coeval with China and Egypt, the three constituting the most ancient civilizations of the world. While Western Europe was still the abode of barbarians, and while even Greece had scarcely felt the impulse which aroused her to intellectual life, the fabrics of India had reached a marvelous degree of fineness and beauty; and the monarchs of the West counted it a great privilege to be clothed in the "purple and fine linen" of the Orient.

EARLY HISTORY.

2. The early history of India seems a confused tangle of strifes and contentions between different nations and races for the possession of this region, inexpressibly rich in all that makes a land desirable for the occupation of man, and of wars between local rulers striving for dominion. In the midst of this confusion, however, there seems to be good evidence that the early civilization made its

first appearance in the valleys of the Upper Indus; that all invasions, until recent times, were from the fierce tribes of the table-lands to the northwest; that the industrious people of the valleys were driven from their homes by successive incursions of barbarians, extending through many centuries; that each horde, becoming partially civilized, was in turn driven forward; and that the migrations were continuous from the north to the south. Thus it happens that at present the population of India consists of at least thirty distinct nationalities, and that the aboriginal possessors of the Vale of Cashmere have been driven forward, until now they are found only upon the summits of the Neilgherry Mountains, in the extreme southern part of the peninsula.

THE MOGUL EMPIRE.

3. The Brahminical religion has prevailed in India from the earliest period. The first literary productions of the people are the Vedas, the sacred books of the Brahmins. This religion is tolerant and inclusive. Its pantheon recognizes so many gods that each barbarous tribe from the North found their own deity represented, so that their crude religious notions readily merged in the more complicated system of the people they had conquered. The great Buddhistic reform spent its force, and, although triumphant in other lands, it left but little impress in India where it originated. The whole people believed the Brahminical creed and practiced the Brahminical precepts. It was a religion that included the purest abstractions and the grossest form of idolatry. While absorbing all other creeds, it never sought to make converts to its own.

4. The later incursions from the northwest were es-

sentially different from their predecessors. The tribes of the table-lands had been converted to the fanatical and proselyting faith of Mohammed. About the middle of the sixteenth century, a Mongol tribe, strong and stalwart from late successful wars, and full of the fierce zeal of recent converts to Moslemism, appeared at the northern gate of India, and in a short time overspread the country and established the Mogul Empire, with its capital at Delhi. The stern conquerors never rested until they had firmly established their authority over the whole country.

5. The first great Sultan, Baber, had a genius for government. He was firm and temperate in his administration, and he protected the common people from the worst rapacity of their former rulers. Out of the chaos of native rule he evoked something like civilized order, and he established the Mogul Empire upon the foundation of a higher form of justice than had ever before been practiced in the East. After a reign of fifty years, this great monarch died in 1605, two years before the adventurous John Smith set foot upon the territory of Virginia.

6. For another hundred years, the Mogul Emperors, descendants of Baber, held firm possession of India, and in that time the country reached the height of its power in wealth and influence. Temples and palaces, in richness and beauty surpassing the most gorgeous dreams of western-bred people, arose on every side. Arts flourished as never before, and the commerce of India overland to the West was so great that large cities sprung up along its track, solely supported by the trading caravans. The gold from all the nations toward the setting sun was drained to pay for Indian fabrics, and India became the richest country of the world.

7. In the beginning of the eighteenth century the

Mogul Empire began to decline. Weak and effeminate monarchs occupied the throne of Baber and Shah Jehan. The governors of great provinces, while ruling under the name of the Mogul, became really independent, and in turn sub-provinces revolted and set up an independent rule. From 1700 to 1750, the whole country was ablaze with civil war. Rapacious chieftains plundered the people, the arts declined, industry of all kinds languished, and the country upon which Nature had lavished her richest blessings seemed to be surrendered hopelessly to oppression and misrule.

EUROPEAN SETTLEMENTS IN INDIA.

8. During the last century of the Mogul rule, and the following half century of anarchy, a new element entered into the affairs of India, which was destined to effect great and revolutionary changes. Following the wake of Vasco da Gama, the maritime powers of Western Europe all entered into a trade with India by the way of the Cape of Good Hope. The long caravan route through Central Asia was abandoned, and ships of the sea took the place of ships of the desert. Lisbon, Amsterdam, and London absorbed the trade which had made Bagdad, Aleppo, and Bassorah opulent, and these renowned cities of Haroun al-Rashid speedily declined in wealth, power, and influence. The Portuguese, Dutch, French, and English entered into eager competition to secure the trade of India by the new route, and, to facilitate commercial operations, stations called factories were established along the coast. By the consent of the native princes, these factories and a small territory adjacent were under the exclusive civil control of the people occupying them.

9. For a hundred and fifty years these factories re-

Street Scene in Calcutta.

mained mere trading stations, taking no part in the general political affairs of the country. While trade was active, and the profits great, the East India Companies who controlled the factories were content; and, while the annual tribute or rent was paid with regularity, the native princes had a strong motive for protecting the trading companies in their operations. But the display of barbaric splendor excited the cupidity of many of the agents of the companies, and the atrocities of barbaric tyranny aroused the indignation of others, and there came a time when interference in native affairs seemed both natural and proper.

10. The time of the new departure in policy was about the middle of the eighteenth century; the place, the southeast coast; and the occasion, the civil wars which grew out of disputed succession. The student of history finds it difficult to understand fully the political situation at the time. One of the most powerful of all the provinces of the Mogul Empire was "The Deccan," which extended its sway over all of Southern India. The ruler, known as the "Nizam," administered the government in the name of the Mogul, but in reality he was independent, and a true Eastern despot. The chief province of the Deccan was "The Carnatic," which embraced all the territory along the eastern coast. The sovereign of this region, called the "Nabob," while paying a nominal tribute to the Nizam, was really independent, raising revenue, waging wars, and forming alliances without reference to either the government of the Deccan or that of the Mogul Empire.

11. To add to the general confusion, bands of Mahrattas, in numbers forming large armies, were constantly roaming through the country, and levying contributions on both the governments and the people. This peculiar

race was at first a mere band of robbers, which descended from the western mountains of India, but by repeated conquests, and by accessions from the wild and turbulent classes of all parts of the country, they had become a great power, and ruled in many fertile provinces. "In becoming sovereigns, they did not cease to be freebooters. Every region which was not subject to their rule was wasted by their incursions. Whenever their kettle-drums were heard, the peasant threw his bag of rice on his shoulder, hid his small savings in his girdle, and fled with his wife and children to the mountains or the jungles, to the milder neighborhood of the hyena and the tiger."

DUPLEIX AND FRENCH POLICY.

12. At this time the two principal factories on the east coast of India were the British station at Fort St. George, now Madras, and the French station at Pondicherry, eighty miles farther south. The first man who seems to have entertained definite notions about building up a European sovereignty upon the ruins of the Mogul Empire was Dupleix, the French Governor at Pondicherry. His long residence in the East had given him a knowledge of Indian affairs that few Europeans possessed. "His restless, capacious, and inventive mind," says Macaulay, "had formed this scheme at a time when the oldest servants of the English Company were busied only about invoices and bills of lading. Nor had he only proposed for himself the end. He had also a just and distinct view of the means by which it was to be attained.

13. "He clearly saw that the greatest force which the princes of India could bring into the field would be no match for the small body of men trained in the discipline and guided by the tactics of the West. He saw,

also, that the natives of India might, under European commanders, be formed into armies such as Saxe or Frederick would be proud to command. He was perfectly aware that the most easy and convenient way in which a European adventurer could exercise sovereignty in India was to govern the motions, and speak through the mouth, of some glittering puppet dignified by the title of Nabob or Nizam. The arts, both of war and policy, which a few years later were employed with such signal success by the English, were first understood and practiced by this ingenious and aspiring Frenchman."

14. In 1748 the Nizam of the Deccan died. Two claimants for the throne appeared in the persons of Nazir Jung, son of the old Nizam, and Mirzapha Jung, a grandson. About the same time an adventurer, Chunda Sahib, set up a claim for the throne of the Carnatic against Anaverdy Khan, the reigning prince. Here was the opportunity for Dupleix to carry his long-cherished plans into execution. He espoused the cause of Chunda Sahib in the Carnatic, and sent four hundred French soldiers to his assistance. A battle was fought and Anaverdy Khan was killed. His son Mohammed Ali fled with a scanty remnant of his army to Trichinopoly, and nearly all the Carnatic submitted to the conqueror.

15. Next Dupleix lent his French soldiers to Mirzapha Jung, who in a short time became master of the Deccan. The new sovereigns showered wealth and favors upon the successful Frenchman. He was declared governor of a territory in India as large as all France, with a population of 50,000,000 people. He was placed in command of the largest military force of the country. He was presented with a million dollars in money and many valuable jewels. Neither the Nizam nor the Nabob concluded any affairs of moment without his advice

and consent. He was, in fact, invested with sovereign powers, and French influence in Southern India was paramount and seemingly firmly established.

16. The triumph of the French arms carried consternation to the British factory at St. George. Unless the victorious career of Dupleix could be stayed, not only would British influence be destroyed, but the very existence of their trading posts would soon be at an end. At this time the government of St. George was feeble. The military officers in command were without experience. Everything betokened speedy and irretrievable ruin. In this emergency the valor and genius of an obscure English youth suddenly turned the tide of fortune.

ROBERT CLIVE AND THE SIEGE OF ARCOT.

17. Robert Clive had gone to India in the service of the company as commissary to the soldiers stationed at Fort St. George. His duties were those of a clerk. He was now twenty-five years old, but had had no experience in military affairs. Like Dupleix, however, he seemed to comprehend the political situation of the country, and when the emergency came that called forth his powers, he was found to possess both military genius and profound statesmanship. He represented to the officers of the post that if Trichinopoly, now besieged by Chunda Sahib and his French allies, should surrender, Mohammed Ali would perish, and French influence would become supreme. As the distance of Trichinopoly from Fort St. George was so great as to preclude the possibility of marching directly to the assistance of their ally, he advocated the bold project of making a diversion by a sudden attack upon Arcot, the capital of the Carnatic, and the favorite residence of the Nabob. His plans were ap-

proved, and he was appointed commander to carry them into execution.

18. "The young captain," says Macaulay, "was put at the head of two hundred English soldiers and three hundred sepoys, armed and disciplined after the English fashion. The weather was stormy, but Clive pushed on through thunder, lightning, and rain, to the gates of Arcot. The garrison in a panic evacuated the fort and the English entered it without a blow. Clive immediately began to collect provisions, to throw up works, and make preparations for sustaining a siege. The garrison, which had fled at his approach, had now recovered from its dismay, and, re-enforced to the number of three thousand men, it encamped close to the town. At dead of night Clive marched out of the fort, attacked the camp by surprise, slew great numbers, dispersed the rest, and returned to his quarters without having lost a single man.

19. "The news of the fall of Arcot soon reached Chunda Sahib, as he was besieging Trichinopoly. An army under the command of his son Rajah Sahib, numbering ten thousand native troops and one hundred and fifty Frenchmen, was immediately dispatched to Arcot, and proceeded to invest the fort, which seemed quite incapable of sustaining a siege. The walls were ruinous and the ditches dry. The garrison, reduced by casualties, now consisted of one hundred and fifty English soldiers and two hundred sepoys. The stock of provisions was scanty, and the commander was a youth of five and twenty, who had been bred a book-keeper.

20. "During fifty days the siege went on. During fifty days the young captain maintained the defense with a firmness, vigilance, and ability which would have done honor to the oldest marshal in Europe. The garrison

began to feel the pressure of hunger. At this juncture the sepoys came to Clive, not to complain of their scanty fare, but to propose that all the grain should be given to the Europeans, who required more nourishment than the natives of Asia. The thin gruel, they said, which was strained away from the rice, would suffice for themselves. The devotion of Clive's little band equaled that of the Tenth Legion of Cæsar, or of the Old Guard of Napoleon.

21. "Clive looked for succor from two sources. An attempt made by the government at Madras to relieve the place failed, but there was still hope from another quarter. A body of six thousand Mahrattas, under a chief named Morari Row, had been hired to assist Mohammed Ali; but as the French power seemed irresistible, this force had hitherto remained inactive on the frontiers of the Carnatic. The fame of the defense of Arcot roused them from their torpor. Rajah Sahib learned that the Mahrattas were in motion. It was necessary for him to be expeditious. He first offered large bribes to Clive, and vowed that if his proposals were not accepted he would instantly storm the fort and put every man to the sword. Clive told him in reply that his father was a usurper and that his army was a rabble, and that he would do well to think twice before he sent such poltroons into a breach defended by English soldiers.

22. "Rajah Sahib determined to storm the fort. The day was well suited to a bold military enterprise. It was the great Mohammedan festival which is sacred to the memory of Hosein the son of Ali. The history of Islam contains nothing more touching than the event which gave rise to that solemnity. The mournful legend relates how the chief of the Fatimites, when all his brave followers had perished round him, drank his last draught of water

and uttered his latest prayer; how the assassins carried his head in triumph, smote the lifeless lips with his staff, and how a few old men recollected with tears that they had seen those lips pressed to the lips of the prophet of God.

23. "After the lapse of near twelve centuries, the recurrence of this solemn season excites the fiercest and saddest emotions in the bosoms of the devout Moslems of India. They work themselves up to such agonies of rage and lamentation that some, it is said, have given up the ghost from the mere effect of mental excitement. They believe that whoever, during this festival, falls in arms against the infidels, atones by his death for all the sins of life, and passes at once to the Garden of the Houris. It was at this time that Rajah Sahib determined to assault Arcot. Stimulating drugs were employed to aid the effect of religious zeal, and the besiegers, drunk with enthusiasm, drunk with bang, rushed furiously to the attack.

24. "Clive had received secret intelligence of the design, had made his arrangements, and, exhausted by fatigue, had thrown himself on his bed. He was awakened by the alarm, and was instantly at his post. The enemy advanced, driving before them elephants whose foreheads were armed with iron plates. It was expected that the gates would yield to the shock of these living battering-rams. But the huge beasts no sooner felt the English musket-balls than they turned round and rushed furiously away, trampling on the multitude which had urged them forward. A raft was launched on the water which filled one part of the ditch. Clive, perceiving that his gunners at that post did not understand their business, took the management of a piece of artillery himself, and cleared the raft in a few minutes.

25. "Where the moat was dry the assailants mounted

with great boldness; but they were received with a fire so heavy and so well directed that it soon quelled the courage even of fanaticism and intoxication. The rear ranks of the English kept the front ranks supplied with a constant succession of loaded muskets, and every shot told on the living mass below. After three desperate onsets, the besiegers retired behind the ditch.

26. "The struggle lasted about an hour. Four hundred of the assailants fell. The garrison lost only five or six men. The besieged passed an anxious night, looking for a renewal of the attack. But when day broke the enemy were no more to be seen. They had retired, leaving the English several guns and a large quantity of ammunition.

27. "Clive immediately began offensive operations. Re-enforced by seven hundred English troops and sepoys from Madras, and effecting a junction with the auxiliary Mahratta force, he soon overran all the Northern Carnatic. He gained a complete victory over Rajah Sahib's army of five thousand natives and three hundred Frenchmen. At this time Major Lawrence arrived from England and assumed the command. An expedition marched to the assistance of Mohammed Ali at Trichinopoly. The besiegers were defeated, and Chunda Sahib was put to death by the Mahrattas, into whose hands he fell.

28. "The English were now masters of the Carnatic, and the French influence was broken. Steadily the English power was extended over the Deccan and all Southern India. Dupleix struggled against his fate in vain, no French armament came to his assistance. His company condemned his policy and furnished him with no aid. But still he persisted, bribed, intrigued, promised, lavished his private fortune, and everywhere tried to raise new enemies to the government at Madras, but

all to no purpose. At length, when his last hope for empire died out, broken in fortune and spirits, he returned to his native country to die obscure and neglected.

29. "Clive went back to England for a brief space, but after a year or two he returned to India as governor of Madras. His first service after his return was to rout out a nest of pirates which had for a long time maintained a stronghold upon the coast. He then turned his attention to reform in the company's business, and to strengthening British influence with the natives in all directions. Before two months had expired he received intelligence which called forth all the energies of his bold and active mind.

THE STORY OF THE BLACK HOLE.

30. "Of the large provinces into which the Mogul Empire was divided the wealthiest was Bengal. No part of India possessed such natural advantages, both for agriculture and commerce. The Ganges, rushing through a hundred channels to the sea, has formed a vast plain of rich mold which, even under the tropical sky, rivals the verdure of an English April. The rice-fields yield an increase such as is elsewhere unknown. Spices, sugar, vegetable oils are produced with marvelous exuberance. The rivers afford an inexhaustible supply of fish. The desolate islands along the sea-coast, overgrown with noxious vegetation and swarming with deer and tigers, supply the cultivated districts with salt. The great stream which fertilizes the soil is at the same time the chief highway of Eastern commerce. On its banks, and on those of its tributary waters, are the wealthiest marts, the most splendid capitals, and the most sacred shrines of India. In numbers its inhabitants exceed 60,000,000;

a population greater than that of England and France combined.

31. "The race by which this rich tract was peopled, enervated by a soft climate and accustomed to peaceful employments, bore the same relation to other Asiatics which the Asiatics generally bear to the bold and energetic children of Europe. Whatever the Bengalee does, he does languidly. His favorite pursuits are sedentary. He shrinks from bodily exertion, and, though voluble in dispute and able in the war of chicane, he seldom engages in a personal conflict, and scarcely ever enlists as a soldier. There never, perhaps, existed a people so thoroughly fitted by nature and by habit for a foreign yoke.

32. "The great commercial companies of Europe had long possessed factories in Bengal. The French, the Dutch, and the English had stations on the Hoogly, the chief branch of the Ganges. Of these the English Fort William, on the site of the present city of Calcutta, was nearest the sea. A church and ample warehouses rose in the vicinity, a row of spacious houses, belonging to the chief officers of the East India Company, lined the banks of the river, and in the neighborhood had sprung up a large and busy native town. For the ground on which the settlement stood, the English paid rent to the government, and were permitted to have practical control of their own domain.

33. "The province of Bengal had long been governed by a viceroy of the Mogul, who had become practically independent. In 1756 the sovereignty descended to a youth under twenty years of age, who bore the name of Surajah Dowlah. Oriental despots are perhaps the worst class of human beings, and this unhappy boy was one of the worst specimens of his class. His understanding was naturally feeble, and his temper unamiable. His educa-

tion had been such as would have enervated even a vigorous intellect, and perverted even a generous disposition. He was unreasonable, because nobody ever dared to reason with him, and selfish, because he had never been made to feel himself dependent on the good will of others.

34. "Early debauchery had unnerved his body and his mind. He indulged immoderately in the use of ardent spirits, which inflamed his weak brain almost to madness. His chosen companions were flatterers sprung from the dregs of the people. It is said that he had arrived at the last stage of human depravity, when cruelty becomes pleasing for its own sake, when the sight of pain as pain is an agreeable excitement. It had early been his amusement to torture beasts and birds, and when he grew up he enjoyed with still greater relish the misery of his fellow-creatures.

35. "From a child Surajah Dowlah had hated the English. It was his whim to do so; and his whims were never opposed. He had formed a very exaggerated notion of the wealth which might be obtained by plundering them, and his feeble mind could not perceive that the riches of Calcutta, however great, could not compensate him for what he must lose if the European trade should be driven by his violence to some other quarter. Pretexts for a quarrel were readily found, and Surajah Dowlah marched with a great army against Fort William.

36. "The servants of the company at Madras had been forced to become statesmen and soldiers. Those in Bengal were still mere traders, and were in no condition to defend themselves against the formidable attack. The fort was taken, after a feeble resistance, and nearly the whole English population fell into the hands of the conqueror. A few, including the governor, had saved themselves by taking refuge in the ships. The Nabob seated

himself with regal pomp in the principal hall of the factory and ordered Mr. Holwell, the first in rank among the prisoners, to be brought before him. His Highness talked about the insolence of the English, and grumbled at the smallness of the treasure he had found; but he promised to spare their lives, and retired to rest.

37. "Then was committed that great crime, memorable for its singular atrocity, memorable for the terrible retribution by which it was followed. The English captives were left to the mercy of the guards, and the guards determined to secure them for the night in the prison of the garrison, a chamber known by the fearful name of the Black Hole. The space was only twenty feet square. The air-holes were small and obstructed. It was the summer solstice, the season when the fierce heat of Bengal can scarcely be rendered tolerable to natives of England by lofty hills and by the constant waving of fans.

38. "The number of prisoners was one hundred and forty-six, and they were driven into the cell at the point of the sword. They cried for mercy. They strove to burst the door. Holwell offered large bribes to the jailers; but the answer was that nothing could be done without the Nabob's orders, and that the Nabob was asleep and would be angry if anybody waked him. Then the prisoners went mad with despair, and fought for places near the windows where they might obtain air. The jailers in the mean time held lights at the bars and shouted with laughter at the frantic struggles of their victims.

39. "At length the tumult died away in low gaspings and moanings. The day broke. The Nabob had slept off his debauch, and permitted the door to be opened. Twenty-three ghastly figures staggered out of the charnel-house, one hundred and twenty-three bodies were hastily thrown into a pit and covered up, and the Black Hole of

Calcutta has gone into history as a synonym for all that is dreadful and all that is possible in human suffering.

40. "The horror which daylight revealed awakened neither pity nor remorse in the bosom of the savage Nabob. He inflicted no punishment on the murderers. He showed no tenderness to the survivors. He sent letters to the Court of Delhi, describing his conquest in most pompous language. He placed a garrison at Fort William, and forbade Englishmen to dwell in the neighborhood.

CLIVE IN BENGAL.

41. "In August the news of the fall of Calcutta reached Madras, and excited the fiercest and bitterest resentment. The cry of the whole settlement was for vengeance. Within forty-eight hours after the arrival of the intelligence it was determined that an expedition should be sent to the Hoogly, and that Clive should be at the head of the land forces. The naval armament was under the command of Admiral Watson. Nine hundred English infantry and fifteen hundred Sepoys sailed to punish a prince who ruled over 60,000,000 of people. In October the expedition sailed; but it had to make its way against adverse winds, and did not reach Bengal until December.

42. "In the mean time the Surajah Dowlah was reveling in fancied security. He was so ignorant of the state of foreign countries that he often used to say that there were not ten thousand men in all Europe, and it never occurred to him that it was possible that the English would dare to invade his dominions. But while in no fear of the English, he began to miss them greatly. His revenues fell off, and his ministers at length made him understand that it was more profitable to protect traders than to

plunder them. He was disposed to permit the company to resume their operations when he heard of the arrival of Clive in the Hoogly. He instantly marched with his troops toward Calcutta.

43. "Clive commenced operations with his usual vigor. He routed the garrison at Fort William, recovered Calcutta, and stormed and sacked the Nabob's stations along the river. The Nabob, alarmed at this proof of power and spirit, made overtures of peace. He offered to restore the factory, and to give compensation to those whom he had despoiled.

44. "Clive, considering the disparity of his force and the uncertainty of war, consented to negotiate. The terms which he demanded were those which guaranteed much greater power to the English than they ever had before. His manner was cool and determined, as though conscious of possessing power sufficient to enforce his demands. The Nabob behaved with all the faithlessness of an Indian statesman and with all the levity of a boy. He promised, retracted, hesitated, evaded. At one time he advanced with his army in a threatening manner toward Calcutta, but when he saw the resolute front which the English presented, he fell back in alarm, and consented to make peace on their own terms.

45. "The treaty was no sooner concluded than he formed new designs against them. He intrigued with the French upon the Hoogly. He invited the French force in the Deccan to come and drive the English out of Bengal. All this was well known to Clive and Watson. They resolved to rid themselves of one source of danger before the Nabob's plans were consummated. They attacked the French factory upon the Hoogly. Watson directed the expedition by water, and Clive by land. Their success was rapid and complete. The fort, the

garrison, the artillery, the military stores, all fell into the hands of the English. Fresh from this victory Clive returned to his negotiations with the Surajah Dowlah.

46. "The Nabob was confounded by this sudden movement and the destruction of the French power. He regarded the English with still greater fear and still greater hatred. He oscillated between servility and insolence. One day he sent a large sum to Calcutta, as part of the compensation due for the wrongs he had committed. The next day he sent valuable jewels to Bussy, the French commander in the Deccan, imploring that officer to hasten and protect Bengal against Clive, whom 'may all bad fortune attend.' He ordered his army to march against the English. He countermanded his orders. He tore Clive's letters. He sent answers in the most florid language of compliment. He threatened to impale Mr. Watts, the English agent. He sent for Mr. Watts and begged pardon for the insult.

47. "In the mean time his folly, his vices, his dissolute manners, and his love of low company disgusted all classes of his own subjects, and a formidable conspiracy was formed against him in his own capital. The conspirators entered into negotiation with Clive, and he agreed to place Meer Jaffier, the head of the movement, upon the throne of Bengal. In his diplomacy Clive seems to have laid aside his character as a bluff soldier, and to have taken lessons from his wily and treacherous Indian foes. He intrigued and deceived until the last moment, when the conspiracy was ripe and his army ready.

48. "The moment for action came. Mr. Watts, the English agent, secretly fled and took refuge in Calcutta. Clive put his troops in motion, and wrote to the Nabob a letter in which he set forth the English wrongs, and concluded by saying that, as the rains were about to set in,

he and his men would do themselves the honor of waiting upon his Highness for an answer.

49. "Surajah Dowlah instantly assembled his whole force and marched to encounter the English. It had been arranged that Meer Jaffier should separate himself from the Nabob, and carry over his division to Clive. But as the decisive moment approached, the fears of the conspirator overcame his ambition. Clive advanced to the river which separated him from his foe. The Nabob lay with a mighty power a few miles off at Plassey. Meer Jaffier delayed, and returned evasive answers to the remonstrances of the English general.

THE BATTLE AND ITS RESULTS.

50. "Clive was in an anxious and painful situation. He could place no confidence in the sincerity or the courage of his confederate; and whatever confidence he might have in his own military talents, and in the valor and discipline of his troops, it was no light thing to engage an army twenty times as numerous as his own. Before him lay a river over which it was easy to advance, but over which, if things went ill, not one of his little band would return.

51. "On this occasion, for the first and for the last time, his dauntless spirit, during a few hours, shrank from the fearful responsibility of making a decision. He called a council of war. The majority pronounced against fighting, and Clive declared his concurrence with the majority. Long afterward he said that he had never called but one council of war, and that if he had taken their advice the British would never have been masters of Bengal. But scarcely had the meeting broke up than he was himself again. He retired alone under the shade of some trees,

and passed an hour there in thought. He came back determined to take the risk, and gave orders that all should be in readiness for passing the river on the morrow.

52. "The river was passed; and, at the close of a toilsome day's march, the army, long after sunset, took up its quarters in a grove of mango-trees near Plassey, within a mile of the enemy. Clive was unable to sleep; he heard through the night the sound of drums and cymbals from the vast camp of the Nabob. It is not strange that even his stout heart should now and then have sunk, when he reflected against what odds, and for what a prize, he was in a few hours to contend.

53. "Nor was the rest of Surajah Dowlah more peaceful. His mind, at once weak and stormy, was distracted by wild and horrible apprehensions. Appalled by the greatness and nearness of the crisis, distrusting his captains, dreading every one who approached him, dreading to be left alone, he sat gloomily in his tent, haunted, a Greek poet would have said, by the Furies of those who had cursed him with their last breath in the Black Hole.

54. "The day broke—the day which was to decide the fate of India. At sunrise the army of the Nabob, pouring through many openings of the camp, began to move toward the grove where the English lay. Forty thousand infantry, armed with firelocks, pikes, swords, bows and arrows, covered the plain. They were accompanied by fifty pieces of ordnance of the largest size, each tugged by a long team of white oxen, and each pushed on from behind by an elephant. Some smaller guns, under the direction of French soldiers, were perhaps more formidable.

55. "The cavalry were fifteen thousand, drawn from the bolder races which inhabit the northern provinces; and the practiced eye of Clive could perceive that the

men and horses were more powerful than those of the Carnatic. The force opposed to this great multitude consisted of only three thousand men; but of these, nearly one thousand were English, and all were led by English officers and trained in the English discipline.

56. "The battle commenced with a cannonade, in which the artillery of the Nabob did scarcely any execution, while the field-pieces of the English produced great effect. Several officers in Surajah Dowlah's service fell. Disorder began to spread through his ranks. His own terror increased every moment. One of the conspirators advised him to retreat. This advice, agreeing as it did with what his own terrors suggested, was readily received. He ordered his army to fall back, and this order decided his fate. Clive snatched the moment, and ordered his troops to advance.

57. "The confused and dispirited multitude gave way before the onset of disciplined valor. No mob attacked by regular soldiers was ever more completely routed. The little band of Frenchmen, who alone ventured to confront the English, were swept down the stream of the fugitives. In an hour the forces of Surajah Dowlah were dispersed, never to re-assemble. Only five hundred of the vanquished were slain; but their camp, their guns, their baggage, innumerable wagons, innumerable cattle, remained in the power of the conqueror. With a loss of twenty-two soldiers killed and fifty wounded, Clive had scattered an army of sixty thousand men, and had subdued an empire larger and more populous than Great Britain."

58. This brilliant success of Clive added Plassey as one of the battle-fields of the world which has shaped national destinies and decided the fate of millions of people. Though much was yet to be done before the fruits of

victory could be fully realized, Clive at once became almost supreme in authority. Surajah Dowlah fled in disguise, and disappeared from history in complete obscurity. Meer Jaffier held Clive in slavish awe. He once reproved a native of high rank for some trouble with the company's Sepoys. "Are you yet to learn," he said, "who Colonel Clive is, and in what station God has placed him?" The answer was: "I affront the colonel! I who never get up in the morning without making three low bows to his jackass!"

59. The policy inaugurated by Clive was continued by his successors. The British rule was extended by setting up native princes, or setting them aside, as expediency dictated, until the whole vast region south of the Himalayas passed under their control. The weak trading companies of 1755 have blossomed out into an empire.

60. British India to-day, in extent of territory and in absolute safety, is immeasurably greater than that of the Moguls in the height of their glory. The first wild exercise of irresponsible power has been corrected, and governmental affairs under British rule are now administered on the foundation of substantial justice. The peasant no longer flies from governmental officers to the more merciful companionship of the cobra and tiger, and all who toil find protection as never before. The races of the Orient have been brought face to face with the arts and sciences of the West, and untold millions have cause to bless the day when Robert Clive was forced to close the ledger and take up the sword.

CHAPTER X.

LEXINGTON AND BUNKER HILL.

1. The Pilgrims had passed away. Long years had elapsed since the last of the New England fathers had exchanged the earthly for the heavenly kingdom. The grandchildren and the great-grandchildren of the first immigrants possessed the soil. No aliens they, seeking a refuge in an unknown land, but the sturdy possessors of homes where they were born, and around which clustered all tender family ties. The passionate love for England, filtered through three generations, had moderated to a filial respect without impairing filial obedience.

2. Marvelous the change in outward conditions of that century and a half! Wave after wave of intelligent activity had passed over the land. Settlers' fires hunted the track of Indians westward bound. On the site of primeval forests, fields of grain shimmered in the sun. The rude hut, hastily built for shelter, had given place to the comfortable farm-house and the elegant mansion. Village and city had grown up in the centers of trade. The mechanic arts had slowly made their way. Change vast, weighty, permanent—not sudden, but orderly growth—fruit of seed sown, but none the less marvelous for that.

3. Internal change had accompanied the external. Spiritual growth had gone hand in hand with increase of life's comforts. Persecution as a means of conversion had

disappeared before common dangers and sufferings. Intolerance had toned down into a mild form of bigotry. The shovel-hat of the parson and the flowing robes of the magistrate had lost much of their superstitious significance. The hard, self-imposed restraints of the Puritans had become less rigid at home and in public. Individual life was freer, fuller, and more complete.

4. So sped the years until after the French war—until the last of England's rivals had been effectually subdued. Now England, for the first time, seems to have been brought face to face with her sturdy offspring. Now she deliberately made up her mind to make him useful—pay her debts, fight her enemies, subserve her interests first and always. So, with blustering words about rights, she imposed burdens, with significant hints in regard to chastisements; she withheld privileges; the cherishing mother in word and deed proving to be a veritable step-mother with the hardest of hearts.

5. Here trouble began. The son had an equal share with the parent in Agincourt and *Magna Charta*. He was confiding and unsuspicious, but the experience of three generations in the wilds had accustomed him to freedom, and had given him hardihood. His shoulders were broad, but it was difficult to bind burdens upon them against his will. As the policy of the parent dawned upon him, first came incredulous questioning, "What does this mean?"—then protest, showing the injury and suggesting "There must be some mistake!"—last, conviction of intended injustice, the hot wrath, and the emphatic statement, "I will not obey!" The angry note of defiance was heard rolling along the Atlantic coast from New England to Georgia. Descendants of Roundheads, Cavaliers, and Huguenots forgot their ancient prejudices and united against this common danger.

Patrick Henry responded to the sentiments of Otis and Adams, and Virginia sent friendly greetings to the commonwealth of Massachusetts.

6. The madness that afflicted the last years of the life of George III seems to have taken possession of the British ministry. Exaction followed exaction in increasing intensity and number. The history of coercive legislation can scarcely find a parallel to that of the British Parliament for the fifteen years following the fall of Quebec. Withal, no excuse was ever made for injustice done, no sympathy was ever expressed for suffering inflicted, but all communication conveyed the stern purpose to subdue. Hungry for affection, the half-grown offspring turned his face toward England for the smallest caress, and the east wind brought back across the Atlantic full in his face the sharp crack of a whip.

7. Then came a period of aggression and resistance. The Stamp Act was passed, but stamps could not be sold, and the lives of stamp-venders became miserable. Soldiers crowded citizens upon Boston Common; citizens mobbed the soldiers; soldiers fired, killing five citizens, and were saved from destruction only by the active interference of the patriot leaders. This affray marked the first shedding of blood, and has gone into history as "The Boston Massacre." Tea was taxed, but the matrons took to catnip and sage, and no tea was sold. Three cargoes of taxed tea were sent into Boston harbor, but a war-whoop was heard; the vessels were boarded by a band of painted savages, tomahawk in hand; the tea-chests were broken up and the tea was thrown into the water. This last act demanded special punishment, and the Boston Port Bill shut up the port of Boston, allowing no ship to go in or out. The sympathetic people of Salem and Marblehead placed wharf and warehouse at the disposal

of Boston merchants, softening the blow as much as possible. Relief to the suffering poor of Boston poured in from all sides, and the British ministry saw that the whole people were making common cause in resistance to oppression.

8. The next step is the vigorous use of the strong arm. Filial love must be forced in by means of bayonets, and affection secured by gunpowder and bullets. A strong force of soldiers under General Gage took possession of Boston. The troops were quartered in the City Hall and other buildings sacred in the eyes of the people to justice and peace. The city government was superseded by the military. Sentinels patrolled the streets. Arbitrary edicts took the place of law. Citizens were interfered with while in the pursuit of private business. For soldiers' insults there was no redress. The leading patriots, John Adams, Joseph Warren, James Otis, John Hancock, and Samuel Adams, were hunted, and a price was set on their heads. Boston was in the strong hands of military power. Outwardly it was subdued, but beneath was a seething fire, ready to burst into flame when the moment for conflagration should arrive.

9. But Massachusetts was aroused. Town and country were one. The war spirit invoked engendered its kind. Committees of Safety were formed in every town. The drum and fife echoed from mountain to valley. The musket of the old war, the shot-gun of the sportsman, and the rifle of the hunter were brought from their resting-places and prepared for use. Forge and hammer were busy in making guns and swords. Minute-men in every hamlet prepared to march on the moment. Nor were the women idle; wheel and loom were busy as never before. The patriot soldier, starting for the front, was clad in serviceable home-spun, prepared by loving

hands, and he departed amid the tears, prayers, and blessings of loving yet steadfast hearts.

10. The General Court of Massachusetts was convened. It was denounced and proscribed by General Gage, but in the eyes of the people its mandates had all the force of law. Taxes were levied and cheerfully paid. The colony was divided into military districts, and each one placed under the command of a competent officer. Powder, arms, and other military stores were collected, and all needful preparations were made for war. The other New England colonies fully shared in the excitement of Massachusetts. The note of alarm spread through the land, and a Continental Congress was called to meet at Philadelphia to consider the policy best to be pursued for the common weal.

11. But General Gage became impatient. He would strike a blow that would at once assert British power and terrify the whole rebel race. The mailed hand must be seen beneath the soft glove. The opportunity was not long wanting. A military depot at Concord, eighteen miles northwest of Boston, he determined to seize. A force of eight hundred men, under Lieutenant-Colonel Smith and Major Pitcairn, was to set out on the evening of April 18th. The patriot leaders were early aware that some movement was on foot, and eager eyes watched for indications of its force and direction. But it was kept a profound secret, and it was not until the troops were upon the march that their destination could be guessed. Let the poet tell how the purpose was discovered and the news carried to the country:

PAUL REVERE'S RIDE

12. Listen, my children, and you shall hear
Of the midnight ride of Paul Revere,
On the eighteenth of April, seventy-five.
Hardly a man is now alive
Who remembers that famous day and year.

13. He said to his friend, "If the British march
By land or sea from the town to-night,
Hang a lantern aloft in the belfry arch
In the North Church tower as a signal light—
One if by land, and two if by sea;
And I on the opposite shore will be,
Ready to ride and spread the alarm
Through every Middlesex village and farm,
For the country folk to be up and to arm."

14. Then he said "Good night!" and with muffled oar
Silently rowed to the Charlestown shore,
Just as the moon rose over the bay,
Where, swinging wide at her moorings, lay
The Somerset, British man-of-war:
A phantom ship, with each mast and spar
Across the moon like a prison bar,
And a huge black hulk, that was magnified
By its own reflection in the tide.

15. Meanwhile his friend, through alley and street,
Watches and wanders, with eager ears,
Till in the silence around him he hears
The muster of men at the barrack door,
The sound of arms, and the tramp of feet,
And the measured tread of the grenadiers,
Marching down to their boats on the shore.

Paul Revere's Ride.

16. Then he climbed the tower of the old North Church,
By the wooden stairs, with stealthy tread,
To the belfry chamber overhead,
And startled the pigeons from their perch
On the somber rafters, that round him made
Masses and moving shapes of shade;
By the trembling ladder, steep and tall,
To the highest window in the wall,
Where he paused to listen and look down
A moment on the roofs of the town,
And the moonlight flowing over all.

17. Beneath in the churchyard lay the dead,
In their night-encampment on the hill,
Wrapped in a silence so deep and still
That he could hear, like a sentinel's tread,
The watchful night-wind as it went
Creeping along from tent to tent,
And seeming to whisper "All is well!"

18. A moment only he feels the spell
Of the place and the hour, and the secret dread
Of the lonely belfry and the dead;
For suddenly all his thoughts were bent
On a shadowy something far away,
Where the river widens to meet the bay—
A line of black that bends and floats
On the rising tide like a bridge of boats.

19. Meanwhile, impatient to mount and ride,
Booted and spurred, with a heavy stride,
On the opposite shore walked Paul Revere.
Now he patted his horse's side,
Now gazed on the landscape far and near,
Then, impetuous, stamped the earth,

And turned and tightened his saddle-girth;
But mostly he watched with eager search
The belfry-tower of the old North Church,
As it rose above the graves on the hill,
Lonely and spectral and somber and still.
And lo! as he looks, on the belfry's height
A glimmer, and then a gleam of light.
He springs to the saddle, the bridle he turns,
But lingers and gazes, till full on his sight
A second lamp in the belfry burns.

20. A hurry of hoofs in the village street,
A shape in the moonlight, a bulk in the dark,
And beneath, from the pebbles in passing, a spark
Struck out by a steed flying fearless and fleet.
That was all! and yet, through the gloom and the light,
The fate of a nation was riding that night;
And the spark struck out by that steed in its flight
Kindled the land into flame with its heat.

21. The British column moved on through the darkness with no sound save the steady tread of marching feet. At first, farm-house and hamlet were wrapped in a deep repose, but as the night wore on signs of life began to appear. At every cross-road, horsemen galloped off at their approach, and hurried lights at chamber windows showed that slumber had been suddenly interrupted. At day-break the invading force reached Lexington, a little village twelve miles from Boston. Here minute-men to the number of about one hundred and twenty, aroused by the cry of Paul Revere, had hastily assembled. They offered no opposition to the British troops, but stood silent spectators to the unusual sight.

THE FIGHT
AT LEXINGTON

22. The British column halted, and Major Pitcairn rode forward, and, in the most peremptory tone of command, cried out: "Disperse, you rebels? Throw down your arms and disperse!" No one obeyed, and he gave the order to fire. Out blazed the muskets, and what remained of the little group sought safety in flight. The British marched on, leaving on that peaceful common, under the very shadow of the church, eight figures stark and motionless in death. From this baptism of blood they moved on, regretful, perhaps, at the stern necessity of their action, but rejoicing that all opposition had been so easily and completely overcome.

23. On they sped. The sun arose in its glory to cheer them on their march. Their thoughts were jubilant as in fancy they posed as heroes before their fellows left behind. No vision of the dead men staring upward from the blood-drenched grass of Lexington haunted them. The silent march of the night had ended, and now they could press onward with clatter and song. The six miles to Concord were soon passed over. A strong guard was left at the bridge, for, with all his confidence, Colonel Smith was a skillful commander, and would neglect no precaution to secure the safety of his troops. So careful was he that he sent back a secret messenger from Lexington for more men. On press the exulting soldiers, on through the streets of Concord in search of the military stores. But lo! they had taken wings and flown to a place of safety. A few barrels of flour, half destroyed, a few hundred cannon-balls thrown into wells, was the sole outcome of the intended destruction. The Committee of Safety had performed their duty discreetly and in time.

24. But hark! What means that musketry? Not the scattering fire of a skirmish, but volley answering volley! Has the impossible come to pass? Have the rebels

dared to fire upon the king's troops? But the firing grows warmer, louder. Hasten to the bridge lest retreat be cut off! The guards, sore beset, welcome the aid. Armed foes spring up on every side! They are behind, before —everywhere! No safety now but in instant, rapid retreat.

25. "You know the rest. In the books you have read,
How the British regulars fired and fled—
How the farmers gave them ball for ball,
From behind each fence and farm-yard wall;
Chasing the red-coats down the lane,
Then crossing the fields, to emerge again
Under the trees, at the bend of the road,
And only pausing to fire and load."

26. Discipline and valor are of no avail here. Vollied musketry has little chance against backwoods sharpshooters occupying every vantage ground that their knowledge of the country enabled them to do. The day was wearing on. Noon found them a disorganized mass, flying through Lexington streets, the scene of their morning victory.

27. In the mean time Lord Percy, with eight hundred fresh troops and two field-pieces, is marching out on the Lexington road; not that any danger was apprehended, but simply as a precautionary measure. Between two and three o'clock, while yet two miles short of Lexington, ominous sounds of conflict smote his ears: not the rolling volleys and stately tread of victory, but the confused noise of fight and flight, betokening irretrievable disaster. The fresh troops were formed into a hollow square, and pell-mell the hunted fugitives came rushing into their place of refuge. Exhausted by their long march and hot fight, many of them fell prone upon the ground, "their tongues," says a high authority, "hanging out of their mouths."

28. But Lord Percy must not delay. Ten miles lie between him and safety, and many hours of day remain before darkness will lend its friendly aid. Short time for rest. Beat off the fierce and persistent attacks! Speed away while yet unsurrounded! A British army must never suffer the humiliation of defeat and capture by a horde of rebel Yankees. So through the afternoon the red-coats marched quickly, sullenly, dejectedly, fighting desperately for very life. The day closed as they neared the river, and under the starlight they embarked, finding safety and rest at last—not quite yet, for as the last boat left the shore a rifle blazed out, and one more victim was sent to atone for the wanton murder on Lexington Common.

29. The eventful day ended with a loss on the part of the British of two hundred and seventy-three, while the aggregate loss of the patriots was one hundred and five. Without discipline, and with the most reckless exposure to danger, they had inflicted a loss nearly three times as great as they had sustained.

30. The news of Lexington spread, everywhere producing wild excitement. The notes of warlike preparation were heard throughout the land. With deliberate purpose General Gage had sown the dragon's teeth, and there literally sprung up a bountiful crop of armed men. Every village and every farm-house helped to swell the number. The remotest hamlet furnished its contingent. In distant Connecticut, gallant old General Putnam heard the news while plowing. Prompt as when he dragged the wolf from its den, he unyoked his oxen, left his plow in the furrow, and, leaping to his saddle, galloped to the fray. Fiery Ethan Allen, at the head of his Green Mountain Boys, was eager to march, but paused to execute that marvelous enterprise which secured for the patriot cause

the formidable fortresses of Ticonderoga and Crown Point, with all their military stores. Day by day the multitude increased, until thirty thousand men were encamped around Boston, from Charlestown Neck to Dorchester.

31. From the evening of the Lexington fight General Gage was shut up in Boston. The patriots kept a strict guard on every road, and no parties were permitted to pass out or provisions to pass in. All supplies for the town came by sea. The officers chafed under the enforced inactivity. They would be done with the ignoble work of defense behind fortifications. They longed for an opportunity to regain the prestige lost on that fatal nineteenth of April. But General Gage was too wise a commander to risk the safety of his army, so he held the impatience of his officers in check and awaited events.

32. The patriot leaders were equally impatient. The enthusiasm of the moment must be turned to good account. The men were all unused to living in camps, and were peculiarly exposed to camp diseases and camp vices. Discipline had not yet counteracted the demoralizing tendencies of army life. The different divisions of the army were ranged under favorite local leaders, and while there was some show of order there was little or no concert of action. It was now the middle of June. Two months had elapsed since Lord Percy was driven back into Boston.. All means to lure General Gage from the town had failed, and an aggressive movement was devised. It was resolved to take a new position threatening the town and the shipping in the port. The place selected was the highland on the Charlestown peninsula known as Bunker Hill, and the time fixed upon for the enterprise the night of June 16th.

33. Eight hundred men armed with shovels and picks

assembled at six o'clock. The movement was known to be a perilous one, and every man felt that he took his life in his hand. President Langdon, of Harvard College, offered prayer with the ancient Puritan fervor. Colonel Prescott took command of the military operations and Colonel Gridley conducted the engineering. In early evening they set out. The march was in profound silence. With suppressed breathing and stealthy tread they made their way—an army of ghosts entering the land of shadows. But the grim faces of the officers and the clinched hands of the men showed more than ghostly purpose. About midnight the march ceased. Clear in the starlight they could see British ship and camp, and could hear the sentinel proclaim, "All is well." A redoubt eight rods square was laid out, and these eight hundred husbandmen bent their seasoned muscles to the work. The embankment grew up in the darkness, and at day-break its six feet of height amply protected the workers within.

34. In the American camp all was excitement and expectation. Supporting parties were organized, supplies hurried up, and means for re-enforcement and retreat provided. It was now that the fatal weakness of the patriot organization was made manifest. Different leaders had notions inconsistent with each other, and divided councils led to indecisive action. The brunt of the coming engagement was left to one tenth of the patriot forces. Scarred veterans scented the battle from afar, and hastened to the front to share the danger and the glory. With no command, officers were content to act as volunteers and handle muskets. Putnam, with military foresight, took charge of the line of communication, and with true farmer instinct he converted two rail-fences and a field of new-mown hay into a line of serviceable

breastworks reaching across Charlestown Neck into the country.

35. At day-break the astonished Britons gazed upon this vision of the night. A moment's pause, then instantaneous, rapid action. That nocturnal growth threatened their very lives. Those audacious and insolent rebels must be swept from existence. Without orders the Boston battery at Copp's Hill opened upon the redoubt as soon as it was discovered. Ships in the bay poured in furious broadsides. The cannonade awoke Boston from her slumbers. Citizens half dressed rushed into the streets. Every roof and steeple that commanded a view of the scene was soon crowded with anxious spectators, who remained there during the livelong day. Patriot and royalist mingled, and fierce passions and wordy wars accompanied the progress of the conflict outside. Exultation at patriot success was often too great to be suppressed, and wild cheers sounded from the house-tops and echoed through the streets.

36. So passed the forenoon. The little band on the hill, protected by the earth-works, worked on with speed and safety. The hurtling masses of iron aimed at their destruction either buried themselves in the yielding earth or passed overhead without injury. One man only paid with his life the penalty of his curiosity in looking over the breastworks. An early luncheon was served and then work again. But even iron muscles have their limit of endurance, and the earth-walls grew less rapidly as the day wore on, until at high noon work altogether ceased.

37. But what of the enemy! By this time they are aware of the uselessness of their cannonade. Other and stronger measures must be taken, and that on the instant. The military renown gained on so many battle-fields must not be lost in a conflict with rude peasants—the

best point of vantage in a general war must not be lost to the king. Every sentiment of ambition and loyalty urged to action. A ship dropped down the river and took position to command Charlestown Neck. But the rail-fence and the new-mown hay resisted the shock, and the American line remained unturned. Rough old Putnam's foresight became an important factor in the day's conflict.

38. Suddenly the drum's loud beat and the shrill scream of the fife startled all hearts into a fiercer life. The notes, with no tremor of fear, rang out sonorous, triumphant. For centuries such notes had led Britons to victory, and to-day British soldiers will do or die. Four thousand grenadiers, under Lord Howe, march down to the shore with the quick, elastic tread of soldiers upon a holiday excursion. In that resolute front and precision of movement there was little to raise the spirits or inspire hope in the hearts of the thousands of patriotic observers who were watching the movements with feverish anxiety. In perfect order they embark, and in perfect order they land upon the Charlestown shore. In their advance toward the silent redoubt no line wavered and no step faltered, though every man was aware of the fearful peril before him.

39. Within the little earth-work all was activity and expectation. Pomeroy, Stark, Putnam came to help—not to dictate. At the last moment General Warren, from the State Committee of Safety, unable to conceal his anxiety, came and took his place in the ranks. These officers all outranked Colonel Prescott, but neither of them would take the command from the officer who had proved himself capable and worthy of it. Shovels and picks gave place to rifles and muskets, and, as experienced eyes glanced along the death-dealing tubes, grave smiles

lit up rugged faces at the thought of the welcome the enemy would soon receive. "Be steady! Be firm!" is the parting injunction of Putnam, as he takes his way to his command at the rail-fence. "We must conquer or die," is the sentiment of Warren, as he grasps the musket of a common soldier, showing to the last that noble patriotism which makes his name so dear to all who love their country. "Keep cool. Wait until you see the color of their eyes! Aim at their red coats. Pick off their commanders!" are the fiery last commands of Prescott, as the scarlet column moved up the hill. Each soldier is in place, each eye unflinchingly is fixed on the enemy, and each right hand is pressed upon the musket, ready for the supreme moment.

40. The batteries, which had been covering the advancing columns, ceased as they neared the summit. An ominous silence succeeded the tumult of the preceding hours. No sound is heard but the short, quick words of command in the British ranks, and the steady tread of the marching files. The space had diminished to a few rods, and still a grave-like silence wrapped the redoubt. At the last moment had the hearts of the patriots failed? Did the near approach of the red-coats deprive them of their courage? "By the double-quick, forward march!" rang out from the British lines. A sudden rush, and one deafening volley! Was it lightning from heaven that struck down every man in their first rank? Was it the earthquake's shock that left those long lines of dead heaped like grass before the mower's scythe? The rear ranks, paralyzed by the terrible disaster, held their ground, but no human courage could withstand the fire that blazed fierce and merciless from the redoubt. A moment's pause, and then a wild, headlong flight to the sheltering boats on the shore.

41. As shouts of triumph went up from thousands of sympathizing hearts, the contending forces were in a state of intense activity. Within the breastworks Prescott, cool, deliberate, masterful, watched every detail and directed every action. Warren, Stark, and Pomeroy put soul into every movement. Putnam defended his own line, and sent the good news outward to cheer the thousands who had taken no part in the contest, and to urge immediate re-enforcements. In the British quarters new officers took the place of those who lay stretched on the hill-side; the men were rallied and reformed; new regiments came over from Boston, and again four thousand men breasted the hill and marched up to the breastworks with colors flying and drums beating. This time they were permitted to come within the reach of friendly greeting, when again a solid sheet of flame leaped forth from the breastworks, again covering the earth with the dead. The rear columns for a few moments stood fast, but nothing could withstand that hail of shot aimed to take life, and again they fled to the shore.

42. The day was wearing on. It was now five o'clock. If the Americans can hold on until the friendly darkness sets in, they may retain possession of Charlestown and force the British to evacuate Boston. General Ward was at Cambridge, trying in vain to secure order in time for action. General Knox ranged up and down the lines, frantically urging the men to follow him to the fray. Putnam, blazing with excitement and fully comprehending the danger, was everywhere animating and urging on the fresh troops. Now he sent almost frantic appeals for powder; now he implored the men in reserve to move at once, and now he rallied his own men to repel the attack upon his own lines. A considerable force was at last rallied to march, but upon reaching Charlestown

Neck the firing from the British ships was so deadly that they dared not venture to cross. In the redoubt was the courage of despair. The powder had given out, and for many of the muskets only a single cartridge remained to meet the coming charge. But all remained firm while the sun slowly sunk in the west.

43. After their second repulse, the force under Lord Howe, cowed and demoralized, refuse to again advance into the jaws of death. The idea is gaining ground that the rebel position is impregnable, and that a wise policy demands that no more blood shall be shed in a vain endeavor to reduce it. The impetuous Sir Henry Clinton refuses to take this view of the situation, and his counsels are heeded. Every military resource at the command of General Gage is now brought into requisition. All the ships in the harbor are ordered to direct their fire upon the fort and the line of communication. New batteries are erected by competent engineers to sweep through the outer breastworks and render them untenable. The reserve forces are ordered up, and every available man is in the ranks. The charge must now be made on every side and the little band of eight hundred literally crushed by numbers. All this and the final charge must be made within the few hours of remaining daylight, or British power is forever at an end in America.

44. At last all preparation ends and the time for action arrives. Shot from the new batteries drive the defenders with severe loss within their interior defenses. The advance of the swarming enemies is met with a feeble, scattering fire in place of the volleyed death of the previous charges. Showers of stones and blows from clubbed muskets greet those who first mount the ramparts; but nothing could resist the last desperate bayonet charge of the British. The defenders of the fort slowly and sul-

lenly retired before the overwhelming numbers of their adversaries. At the last moment Major Pitcairn meets his death, and thus expiates as far as possible his bloody orders at Lexington. At nearly the same moment General Warren, in the very rear of the retreating troops, is shot, sealing with his life his devotion to his country. That the retreating Americans were not annihilated was due to the rail-fence of General Putnam, and to his skill in holding the enemy in check while the flying fugitives found safety in the country.

45. The battle of Bunker Hill is ended. The union jack flies over Prescott's redoubt. Four hundred and fifty patriots and fifteen hundred Britons are killed, wounded, and missing. Eighty-nine British officers—numbers unprecedented—sleep in the dust. Patriot courage and endurance are found to equal patriot enthusiasm. Technically the battle is lost; morally it is won. Where Warren fell a nation is born. The Fourth of July records the fact—Yorktown attests the record. A nation is born—from the Pilgrims inheriting love of freedom, from stout Roger Williams toleration—a nation charged with the sacred mission of organizing human rights upon the basis of human liberty.

THE END.

HISTORY.

Quackenbos's American History for Schools. Accompanied with numerous Illustrations and thirty-six Colored Maps.

Quackenbos's Elementary History of the United States. With numerous Illustrations and Maps. 12mo. 260 pages. Revised edition, cloth.

Quackenbos's Primary History of the United States. Made Easy and Interesting for Beginners. Handsomely illustrated. Child's quarto. 192 pages.

Quackenbos's School History of the United States. From the Earliest Discoveries to the Present Time. Embracing a Full Account of the Aborigines, Biographical Notices of Distinguished Men, and numerous Maps, Plans of Battle-Fields, and Pictorial Illustrations. 12mo. 536 pages.

Quackenbos's Illustrated School History of the World. From the Earliest Ages to the Present Time. Accompanied with eighteen Colored Maps and numerous Engravings. 12mo. 473 pages.

Child's First History of Rome. By Miss E. M. Sewell. 18mo. 255 pages.

Child's First History of Greece. By Miss E. M. Sewell. 18mo. 358 pages.

A History of Greece. From the Earliest Times to the Present. By T. T. Timayenis. With Maps and Illustrations. 2 vols. 12mo.

A Class-Book History of England. Illustrated with numerous Woodcuts and Historical Maps. By the Rev. David Morris, B. A. 12mo. 533 pages.

Markham's History of England. From the Invasion of Julius Cæsar to the Reign of Victoria. Revised by Eliza Robbins. 12mo. 387 pages.

[SEE NEXT PAGE.]

Kohlrausch's History of Germany. From the Earliest Period to the Present Time. 8vo. 487 pages.

Arnold's History of Rome. By THOMAS ARNOLD, D. D. Three volumes in one. 8vo. 670 pages.

Arnold's Lectures on Modern History. With a Preface and Notes, by HENRY REED, M. A., Professor of English Literature in the University of Pennsylvania. Large 12mo. 428 pages.

Greene's History of the Middle Ages. 12mo. 450 pages.

Yonge's Three Centuries of Modern History. Large 12mo.

Taylor's Manual of Ancient History. Containing the Political History, Geographical Position, and Social State of the Principal Nations of Antiquity, and illustrated by the Discoveries of Modern Scholars and Travelers. 8vo. 358 pages.

Taylor's Manual of Modern History. Containing the Rise and Progress of the Principal European Nations, their Political History, and the Changes in their Social Condition; with a History of the Colonies founded by Europeans. 8vo. 312 pages.

Taylor's Manual of Ancient and Modern History. The two foregoing volumes in one. 8vo. 670 pages.

Guizot's History of Civilization in Europe. From the Fall of the Roman Empire to the French Revolution. 12mo. 316 pages.

Mangnall's Historical and Miscellaneous Questions. From the eighty-fourth London edition. With large Additions, embracing the Elements of Mythology, Astronomy, Architecture, Heraldry, etc., by Mrs. JULIA LAWRENCE. Fifth American edition, with a Chapter on the American Constitution. 12mo. 396 pages.

[SEE NEXT PAGE.]

Spalding's History of English Literature. With an Outline of the Origin and Growth of the English Language illustrated by Extracts. 12mo. 413 pages.

English Language and its Early Literature. By J. H. Gilmore, A. M., Professor of Logic, Rhetoric, and English, in the University of Rochester. 12mo. 138 pages.

Latham's Hand-Book of the English Language. 12mo. 398 pages.

Three Centuries of English Literature. By Charles Duke Yonge. 12mo. 649 pages.

Literature Primers. 18mo. vols. Flexible cloth.

Graham's English Synonymes. Classified and explained. With Practical Exercises. Designed for Schools and Private Tuition. With an Introduction and Illustrative Authorities. By Henry Reed, LL. D. 12mo. 344 pages.

Robbins's Class-Book of Poetry. 12mo. 252 pages.

Home Pictures of English Poetry. For Firesides and Schoolrooms. 1 vol., 12mo.

Reid's Dictionary of the English Language. 12mo. 572 pages.

Webster's Quarto Dictionary, unabridged. Thoroughly revised and greatly enlarged and improved. Published by G. & C. Merriam, Springfield, Mass. Price, $12.00. Sold by all booksellers.

Graded Instruction in English. For the Use of Teachers. By Orville T. Bright, Principal of Douglas School, Chicago. 18mo. 80 pages.

APPLETONS' SCHOOL READERS,

BY

WM. T. HARRIS, LL. D., *Sup't of Schools, St. Louis, Mo.*
A. J. RICKOFF, A. M., *Sup't of Instruction, Cleveland, Ohio.*
MARK BAILEY, A. M., *Instructor in Elocution, Yale College.*

CONSISTING OF FIVE BOOKS, SUPERBLY ILLUSTRATED.

Appletons' First Reader. Child's Quarto. 90 pages.

In the First Reader the combined word and phonic methods are admirably developed and carefully graded. In the first 52 pages (Part I), in connection with beautiful and child-life reading-lessons, are taught the names of *all* the letters, the *short* sounds of the vowels, and the sounds of the consonants and diphthongs. In Part II are found a systematic *marking* of silent letters and the *more easily* distinguished sounds of vowels, and a continued drill in the sounds of consonants. The aim is to make the pupil acquainted with the forms and powers of letters, and the sound, construction, and meaning of words. The pictorial illustrations have been made a feature not only of unusual attractiveness, but are instructive and interesting adjuncts to the text, as subjects for study and oral exercises.

Appletons' Second Reader. 12mo. 143 pages.

This continues the plan of the First, and gives a complete table of all the vowel and consonant sounds with their markings according to Webster —"A Key to Pronunciation." Preceding each reading-lesson the new words of that lesson are carefully marked for a spelling-exercise. This Reader gives prominence to the phonic analysis and the noting of silent letters, to the placing of diacritical marks, which must be learned by practice in marking words; also, to the spelling of words and to sentence-making, using the words occurring in the reading-lessons.

Appletons' Third Reader. 12mo. 214 pages.

In this Reader the plan of the second is continued, with the addition of some important features, notably the lessons "How to read," placed at intervals through the book. They form the preliminary instruction in elocution which Professor Bailey has developed in this and the succeeding volumes in a masterly and unique manner.

The selection of "comparatively common words," yet such as are easily and usually misspelled, numbering about five hundred, given at the close, is a feature of very great practical value, and answers beyond cavil the question sometimes asked, "Ought not a speller to accompany or precede the series?"

[SEE NEXT PAGE.]

ENGLISH LANGUAGE, COMPOSITION, AND LITERATURE.

The Child's Book of Language. A Graded Series of Lessons and Blanks, in four numbers, with a Teacher's Edition. By J. H. STICKNEY.

No. 1. STORIES IN PICTURES. No. 3. STUDIES IN PLANTS.
No. 2. STUDIES IN ANIMALS. No. 4. STUDIES OF WORDS.

Letters and Lessons in Language. In Four Parts. By J. H. STICKNEY. A sequel to "The Child's Book of Language."

THE SAME. Book V.—GRAMMAR.

Studies in Language: A Teacher's Guide to "Letters and Lessons in Language. By J. H. STICKNEY.

De Graff's School-room Exercise Books. For Primary Grades. Designed for written spelling, and exercises in the correct use of language, composition, etc. 32 pages.

Quackenbos's First Lessons in Composition. In which the Principles of the Art are developed in Connection with the Principles of Grammar; embracing full directions on the Subject of Punctuation; with Copious Exercises. 12mo. 182 pages.

Quackenbos's Advanced Course of Composition and Rhetoric. A Series of Practical Lessons on the English Language, and the various Departments of Prose and Poetical Composition. Illustrated with Copious Exercises. Adapted to Self-Instruction, and the Use of Schools and Colleges. Revised edition. 12mo. 453 pages.

Bain's English Composition and Rhetoric. American edition, revised. 12mo. 343 pages.

Landmarks of English Literature. By HENRY J. NICOLL. 12mo. 460 pages.

[SEE NEXT PAGE.]

Introductory Fourth Reader. 12mo.

Designed for those pupils who have finished the Third Reader, and are yet too young or too immature to take up the Fourth.

Appletons' Fourth Reader. 12mo. 248 pages.

It is here that the student enters the domain of literature proper, and makes the acquaintance of the standard writers of "English undefiled" in their best style. Having received adequate preparation in the previous books, he is now able to appreciate as well as to assimilate the higher classics now before him.

A new and invaluable feature in the editorship of this and the next volume is the "Preparatory Notes" appended to each selection, for the aid of both teacher and pupil.

The elocutionary work commenced in the Third Reader is continued and gradually advanced to the higher phases of the subject. Spelling-exercises are also appended, introducing "Words difficult to spell," with both phonic and what are usually known as orthographic principles formulated into rules. Beautifully engraved full-page illustrations embellish the interior of the book, and render it artistically chaste and attractive.

Appletons' Fifth Reader. 12mo. 471 pages.

This Reader is the one to which the editors have given their choicest efforts. The elementary principles of the earlier volumes are not forgotten in this, but are subordinated to matters germane to more advanced teaching. The "Preparatory Notes" are more advanced than those of the preceding Reader, and seek to direct the mind more to style and the literary character, and lastly to the logical element of the thought. Literary history and criticism are woven into the work in such way as to evoke thought and inquiry in the mind of the young. Extracts are given from Webster, Jefferson, Irving, Audubon, Cooper, Emerson, Wirt, and Washington, along with others from De Quincey, Goethe, Victor Hugo, Byron, Shelley, Milton, Coleridge, and Shakespeare; and with these is a vast amount of valuable information of every kind. It is, indeed, a text-book of *belles-lettres*, as well as of reading and spelling. Professor Bailey's lessons in elocution are fuller than in preceding volumes, and can probably not be equaled in the language for perspicuous brevity and completeness. All the departments of recitation—the earnest and plain, the noble, the joyous, the sad—sarcasm, scorn, humor, passion, poetry—are given clearly and practically. The collection of "Unusual and Difficult Words" at the close comprises fifty-four lists of words which should always be kept in mind by the student.